WE, the Women of India

Named one of Forbes India's 30 Under 30 in 2017, **Angellica Aribam** is a political activist who has been working on issues of gender, anti-racism, and the democratization of politics for over a decade. Her work has been featured widely by both national and international media. She regularly writes for various newspapers including the *Indian Express* and the *Times of India*. She is committed to amplifying women's leadership in Indian politics.

Akash Satyawali is a public policy professional and joint secretary with the Research Department of the Indian National Congress. He regularly writes for various publications including *Deccan Herald, The Wire* and *The Hindu* on law, economy and public policy.

We, the Women of India

Fifteen Voices That Shaped the Constitution

ANGELLICA ARIBAM & AKASH SATYAWALI

Adapted for children by Vidya Nesarikar

hachette
INDIA

First published in paperback in 2025 by Hachette India
(Registered name: Hachette Book Publishing India Pvt. Ltd)
An Hachette UK company
www.hachetteindia.com

1

Box vector and dingbats by Vecteezy.com

Certain place names, such as Bombay, Calcutta and Madras, among others, as well as the names of certain provinces and presidencies, such as Bengal and Madras, have been used to retain the historicity of the information, as far as possible with new names.

Quotes by the persons written about in the book are featured under Fair Use.

This book has been adapted from the title *The Fifteen*, first published in 2024 by Hachette India.

Subsequent edition/reprint specifications may be subject to change, including but not limited to cover or inside finishes, paper, text colour and/or colour sections.

For sale only in India

ISBN 978-93-5731-714-6

Hachette Book Publishing India Pvt. Ltd
4th & 5th Floors, Corporate Centre
Plot No. 94, Sector 44, Gurugram – 122003, India

Typeset by Manmohan Kumar, Delhi

Printed and bound in India
by Manipal Technologies Limited

MIX
Paper | Supporting responsible forestry
FSC™ C043100

CONTENTS

INTRODUCTION

In the world's most populous country and the largest democracy, the Constitution is extremely important. It affects every public debate, whether about religion, citizenship, law, or gender equality. That's why it is important to understand the people who framed our Constitution, their lives, their struggles and their ideas.

The Constitution defines what our country will be. It provides a framework for the rights people possess, how governments must function and the policies they must adhere to. The preamble to our Constitution begins with '*We the people*'. It is a recognition of the fact that the Constitution has been brought about to reflect the will and aspirations of the people of our country.

India became independent on 15 August 1947. But months before that, the Constituent Assembly was tasked with formulating the Constitution of the newly independent country. It met for the first time on 9 December 1946.

Initially, it had 389 members of which 292 members had been elected through the Provincial Assemblies, ninety-three members nominated by the Princely States, and four members represented the Chief Commissioners' Provinces. After Partition, a separate Constituent Assembly for Pakistan was created. Subsequently, some representatives ceased to be part of the Indian Constituent Assembly and the membership reduced from 389 to 299. These members set about drafting a Constitution that governs us to this day.

1950 was an important year in our history. It was on 26 January 1950 that the Constitution of India came into effect. The Constitution of India reflects the hopes and dreams of the freedom fighters and reformers of that time. The people who helped frame it came from different parts of the country and had diverse experiences.

Still, the Constituent Assembly didn't truly represent all of India – especially when it came to women. Of the 299 members, only fifteen women were part of it, and that number dropped to thirteen after two of them resigned. These women were some of the foremost leaders of the time, involved in the freedom struggle and social reform movements. This book is written to tell the story of these fifteen amazing women who helped build modern India.

Through intense advocacy that spanned decades, the women leaders had a stellar role in ensuring the right to equality. When the Constitution was adopted, every person was guaranteed to be treated equally in matters of voting, employment and citizenship. A lot of rights we take for granted were the result of years of sacrifice by such leaders.

India has been a democracy for more than 70 years. While we have celebrated many successes, women still don't have enough representation in politics. The struggle for their political rights began over a century ago, in 1917, when a group of Indian women asked for the right to vote. Since then, things have improved slowly, but not enough.

Although conversations on gender have become mainstream in the last decade, the reality is that women have often been invisibilized in our history. Before beginning research for *The Fifteen*, the book this current adaptation is based on, we, the authors, would occasionally find mention of women leaders in our history books. We were eager to learn about their contributions in the framing of the Indian Constitution. It soon became a rabbit hole.

But there wasn't much information available about them. So, we started digging deeper, reading books, articles, letters, and even footnotes to piece their stories together.

As we learned more, we felt proud, inspired and sometimes shocked. These women had done so much, yet they were barely mentioned in history books. We felt it was our responsibility to tell their stories.

One special moment was when we read a quote by Renuka Ray, one of the fifteen women. She had written in her memoir:

'Sixty years hence someone, perhaps a woman, looking back will tell the story of how a new movement arose and brought about a social revolution.'

It felt like she had written those words just for us. We kept that quote close to our hearts. And, we have heeded her words and remained as objective as possible.

These women were shaped by their life experiences. Though they came from different backgrounds, they were united by a single goal: to build a better India for future generations.

They faced many challenges – patriarchy, discrimination and societal pressure. Most came from wealthy or influential families, which helped them access education and public life. But Annie Mascarene and Dakshayani Velayudhan were exceptions.

Most of these women were involved in social reform. They worked to end untouchability, stop child marriages, and improve education for women. Many were jailed during the freedom movement. They took on leadership roles in organizations like the All-India Women's Conference (AIWC). They even went to the League of Nations in Geneva to talk about Indian women's right to vote!

Their lives teach us not just about politics and law but also about the different 'Indias' that existed at the time. Their stories are full of struggle, courage and hope. Our attempt, through our writings, has been to show the incredible impact they had – both as individuals and as a group.

We have done our best to tell their stories with respect and care. We hope people will remember them as the giant leaders they were.

1

AMMU SWAMINATHAN

Once in the provisional parliament, in a newly independent India, a feisty lady questioned the Minister of Law, Dr Ambedkar, as to why there were no women in the advisory committee of the Hindu Code Bill – a Bill that dealt with, among other social issues, the property rights of women. The male dominant body erupted into loud laughter.

To the surprise of everyone present, she did not back down – she repeated her question, louder this time. Her assertiveness couldn't be ignored. She meant business and made it known that she was speaking up on behalf of the women of her country. Frivolous laughter from men was the least of her concerns.

'Every time that any question of women's rights comes up in that House, there is general laughter, as if it is a joke. I do not mean it as a joke. I would like the Hon. Law Minister to tell us whether in view of the fact that the Hindu Code

really affects women very largely and there are several women's organizations in India, they have been asked to send representatives to this Advisory Committee that is going to be called very soon.'

She didn't drop the questions till Dr Ambedkar informed her that women's organizations have been invited.

A Mind of Her Own

A.V. Ammukutty, the youngest of thirteen children, was born to a Nair family on 22 April 1894 in Palaghat (now Palakkad) near Kochi, Kerala. She learnt to read and write Malayalam at home. She was taught to cook, in preparation for an early marriage like most girls of the time. But even as a child she questioned gender norms and resented the idea of being tied to only housework. She was described as a 'tomboy' by her mother. When in her teens, she received a marriage proposal from Dr Subbarama Swaminathan – a family friend who hailed from a poor Tamil Brahmin family. Ammu had a few conditions which she put forth boldly. She wanted to move to Madras (now Chennai), learn English from an Englishwoman, and not be asked – 'what time she would reach home', a question that her brothers were never asked.

Subbarama was not shocked, instead he was impressed by Ammu's free spiritedness and readily agreed to all her conditions.

The wedding took place soon after, at the end of 1908, when Ammu was just fourteen years old. (Child marriage was prevalent across India back then. In fact, two decades later, the Child Marriage Restraint Act [also known as Sarda Act] fixed the minimum age of girls for marriage at fourteen. Today, the legal age for marriage in India has been raised to 18 for girls and 21 for boys.)

Despite the age gap of 23 years, it was a match made in heaven. Subbarama was incredibly supportive of Ammu. He was progressive and ahead of his times. A lot of his ideas and actions were similar to Ammu's own ideologies and beliefs.

For instance, while studying, Subbarama received a scholarship to study law at the University of Edinburgh. His relatives were against his plans of going to the United Kingdom on the grounds that crossing the oceans meant that he would lose his 'upper caste' status. Such were the times. But Subbarama paid no heed to the superstitions. Determined, he left for the UK and made the most out of the opportunity by pursuing his passion for both science and law. After obtaining two degrees, the ambitious double graduate obtained a PhD from the University of Harvard, USA.

After returning to India, he continued to reject the diktats of the caste system. He married Ammu despite opposition from his relatives. He was unbothered that she belonged to the Nair community and was not a Brahmin. This was a big deal back in the day.

Ammu in the Driver's Seat!

Immediately after the wedding, Subbarama kept his promise to his bride and the couple moved to Madras. Subbarama was doing well in his career. It was here that Ammu fully came into her own and flourished. There was no one to restrict her. Subbarama was determined to support her with the best opportunities. He also hired an English governess for her. Ammu had her first trip to England, where she stayed with a British family so that she could learn the language better. Here she was introduced to the thrills of theatre. She fully embraced it and began acting in amateur plays. She also began to play tennis. And the cherry on top, she learnt to drive. Cars were rare in the early twentieth century, and it was even more rare to have a woman behind the wheel whizzing around Madras.

Helicopter Parent? Certainly Not!

Ammu and Subbarama had four children – two sons and two daughters – Govinda, Lakshmi, Subbarama Krishna and Mrinalini. The four children had a very British upbringing. Education was given the highest importance. They grew up with governesses, talked in English, and were even trained in British etiquettes. Ammu gave her children a strict upbringing without showing overt affection, but she also gave them the freedom to experience life in their own way, something

TRIVIA TIME!

Captain Lakshmi Sahgal was the commander of Rani of Jhansi Regiment of the Indian National Army (INA), the country's first military regiment for women. She was also a close confidante of Subhas Chandra Bose. Lakshmi's name is etched in the pages of Indian history as a firebrand leader who was taken prisoner in Burma (now Myanmar) during World War II. But only a few know that Lakshmi's strength and courage came from a mother most extraordinary – Ammu Swaminathan.

Captain Lakshmi Sahgal with Subhas Chandra Bose

that she always wanted for herself while growing up. Most importantly, all the children were treated the same without any gender bias – the daughters were not asked what time they were getting home, the same as the boys in the household.

Ammu and Subbarama were truly a beacon of light for the children, and they all turned out to be luminaries in their chosen fields.

Despite a liberal upbringing and their father's high status in legal circles, the Swaminathan children faced caste discrimination from the paternal family. Subbarama and Ammu were shocked when they came to know that their daughters were not allowed to eat inside their Brahmin grandparents' house on visits and had to eat their meals seated on the floor of a verandah.

Such instances did not affect the relationship that Ammu shared with her husband. Her life transformed for the better with his love, support and resources. She was full of dreams and aspirations and wanted to carve her own identity in society. She wanted to crush the stereotype that women only need to be confined to their homes and raise children. She didn't follow traditional rules and lived as a socialite – wearing expensive clothes and jewels, throwing lavish parties and serving Western cuisine to her friends. The who's who of society, including poets, freedom fighters and British aristocrats were all regulars at Ammu's soirées. Although this upset the tradition-bound community, the Swaminathans stood by their choices and embraced their lifestyle confidently.

She was hailed as the 'Queen of Madras'. The most important thing to come out of this was that interacting with people from different walks of life with different perspectives moulded her thinking and laid the foundation for her future social work and political career.

For onlookers, she seemed to have everything – a loving home and a glamourous life. Though many in her position and privilege may have been satisfied being the toast of high society, she wanted more. There was a fire inside her to do something meaningful. Find her purpose. Make her mark. The wheels in her head were turning. Just being a beloved socialite was not enough for her.

Ammu became deeply enthusiastic about politics and the women's movement. This was 1914, and she was all of twenty. Perhaps her exposure to Madras's high society and invigorating conversations on the status of women awakened her desire to work on social reform. Also, some early personal experiences had left a mark on her. Seeing her own mother as a widow, Ammu hated the practices that compelled women to shave their heads, wear white saris, and renounce jewellery upon the death of their husbands. She strongly believed that women were individuals in their own right. Why do they have to look and dress differently if their husband died?

Boss Girls of Yore!

In 1917, she joined hands with forerunners of women's rights movements in India such as British-born Annie Besant, who had made India her home, stalwarts like Kamaladevi Chattopadhyay, Margaret Cousins, Jeena Raja Dasa and Ambujammal to set up the Women's Indian Association (WIA). Their aim was to address the many socio-economic challenges faced by women including child marriage, the devadasi system, widow remarriage, divorce and inheritance. They envisioned a gender-equal future while also working towards expanding equal educational and economic opportunities.

During that time, there were many rumblings in India. Indian reformists were demanding self-rule, i.e., they would still be ruled by the British but with more Indian representatives and other concessions. So, Edwin Montagu was sent to India to make a report of who exactly should be representing India. This was called the Montagu Chelmsford Commission, 1917, and was followed by the Southborough Franchise Committee in 1918. Among other things, this committee was given the task of figuring out who gets the right to vote.

The WIA was part of a combined women's delegation that met the commission and made a compelling case for women's right to vote in elections. Bear in mind, WIA was also India's first national body to advocate for equal voting rights for women. Initially, their demands were rejected citing that the social conditions in India were not ready for women's vote. The British government passed the buck to the provincial governments to decide if women should get the right to vote or not. The women's groups changed tactics and fought for their rights provincially. After a lot of back and forth, and steadfast hard work, in 1919, the Madras Presidency finally gave women the right to vote at the municipal level, but they were still restricted from contesting elections. This was widely criticized. Finally, there was a wind of change. In 1921, women were allowed to contest elections at the local level.

Ammu was in the thick of things and was an active member of the WIA. She would later serve as the vice-president and president of the association. This was a huge recognition and honour for all her contributions. In 1927, the WIA moved to form the All-India Women's Conference (AIWC) alongside other organizations. Ammu continued to be a prominent member. She was one of the fiercest advocates who fought for a legislation to end child marriage, popularly known as the Sarda Bill, a stance only made stronger by the fact that she herself was a child bride.

It was not just women's groups that Ammu was associated with. She was very much part of the Swadeshi Movement in the 1920s. When Mahatma Gandhi called for the mass burning of foreign clothes Ammu couldn't resist the pull of his message.

Carrying on the Battle Alone

Unfortunately, Ammu lost her pillar of support early on in life. Subbarama died in 1930 when Ammu was only thirty-six. True to his character, Subbarama had Ammu taken care of even in death. He didn't want her to follow the customs of widowhood. He also left a will that ensured neither his wife nor his daughters were deprived of inheritances. He bequeathed their family home in Ammu's name. His daughters were to have an equal share in property as his sons. It was truly a remarkable marriage – and having experienced this all through her wedded life, Ammu was all the more determined to advocate equality for all women.

The Work Goes On

Months after her husband's death, Ammu plunged into active politics with a newfound vigour. It was 1930 – the historic year of the Civil Disobedience Movement and the Dandi March. She signed up homemakers for the membership of the Congress. Other than donating time and money, she also put up her home at the complete disposal of the Congress. Many stalwarts of the freedom movement passed through the gates of the residence including Aruna Asaf Ali, Sarojini Naidu and Vijaya Lakshmi Pandit. Her circle was constantly buzzing with women enthusiastic about social reform – passionately challenging the norms.

Ammu continued to divide her time between the Congress and the AIWC. She used the platforms to fight for women's voting rights and argued for equality of women in all spheres, including politics.

Vote for Ammu

In their struggle for women's right to vote, leaders of the women's movement, including Ammu, went abroad to seek support. In 1933, they headed to Geneva to the League of Nations and the International Labour Office. It was highly publicized, garnering a lot of attention and support.

After her return, Ammu contested the Madras Corporation civic polls. She won the election and served from 1934–39. The Government of India Act 1935 (GOI Act 1935) was passed soon after and granted women aged 21 years and above the right to vote nationally. This was a turning point for women in India. This law enabled nearly six million Indian women to vote and also contest elections. Later, this right was also enshrined in the Indian Constitution.

Her work was still not done. She immersed herself in the freedom struggle. She participated actively in the Quit India Movement of 1942. With most of its senior leaders in jail, Ammu donated large sums of money to the Congress to keep the movement going. Using her platform as the president of the AIWC Madras chapter, she also organized strikes and demonstrations. On 19 February 1943, Ammu was arrested and jailed in Vellore for a year for printing and distributing pamphlets with nationalist agenda.

Ammu continued to make advances in her political career. Ammu contested the election for Central Legislative Assembly (equivalent to the present-day Lok Sabha) of 1945 as a Congress candidate. She won from Madras city with 10,883 votes, as opposed to 2,154 for her closest rivals. She managed more than four times the number of votes of her opponent!

WHAT'S IN A NAME?

Plenty, one can say! In India, most surnames give away the caste a person belongs to. So, a name can give a person an unfair advantage or disadvantage based on the hierarchy of the caste one belongs to.

Ammu's indignation at caste supremacy was well known. Ammu once called out Jawaharlal Nehru for using the title of 'Pandit.' And when Nehru pointed out he never asked anyone to call him Pandit, she shot back that he never stopped anyone either.

She had zero tolerance for casteist beliefs perhaps because she and her children had suffered discrimination meted out by her in-laws only because they belonged to another caste.

In another incident from her time at Vellore's Presidency Jail for women, she witnessed a fellow inmate use a casteist slur, *Shudrachi,* to address a female sanitation worker. Annoyed by this, Ammu walked up to the inmate and said, 'Yes, tell me.' The confused inmate explained that she was calling the sanitation worker, to which Ammu replied, 'I am a *Shudrachi* too. Now say what do you want.' The inmate went quiet, taken aback by Ammu's courage.

Soon after, in 1946, she became a member of the Constituent Assembly – the body that was formed to frame the Constitution of India.

Ammu Is a Force to Reckon With

Ammu made her mark in the Constituent Assembly with her rich speeches and fight for women's rights. Back then, Hindu women did not have the right to inherit property if their husbands died without a will. Only sons could do this. There was a lot of buzz on this issue – discussions, bills, and committees were formed. This led Dr B.R. Ambedkar to introduce a draft Hindu Uniform Code in 1948 to remove the legal disabilities that Hindu women suffered and reform Hindu religious laws overall.

There was a lot of opposition from male members who saw it as a breakdown of the Hindu family and culture. Many thought that daughters should not be allowed to inherit property. Ammu was against such thought.

To arrive at an agreement, Dr Ambedkar constituted a select committee of twenty people to go through the draft Bill in order to amend and codify the Hindu Laws. When the body shared its decision after a year, it faced strong opposition again. Nehru then decided to shelve it until the first parliamentary elections. The Hindu Code Bill was finally divided into many segments and passed in Parliament between 1952 and 1956.

Ammu Swaminathan in China with other members of the Congress

Ammu called the Indian Constitution the realization of a great dream of four hundred million people. She reminded the members of the Constituent Assembly that all the rights, ideas and ideals meant nothing if not implemented. Ammu also complained about how long and bulky the Constitution was, having envisioned it as a 'small volume which one could carry in one's purse or pocket'.

Post-Independence she was elected to the first Lok Sabha in 1952. She was one of the twenty-four women elected out of 489 members. She was nominated to serve in the Rajya Sabha from 1957 to 1960. Apart from her time at the Parliament, her interest in movies led her to become the vice-president of the Federation of Film Societies, in 1959.

Ammu also served as India's goodwill ambassador to Russia, China, the USA and Ethiopia.

During 1960–65, she was also the president of the Bharat Scouts and Guides, a voluntary non-political education movement for the youth. She remains the only woman to hold that position in the history of the organization.

Ammu breathed her last on 4 July 1978, at the age of eighty-four. It is hard to put just one tag on her. The essence of her life was that she was always driven to change the status of women in the country. Her life story could have been called a modern-day fairy tale, except it was not a story, it was all true. Her journey from 'tomboy' to 'Queen of Madras' to 'political prisoner' to one of the fifteen women members in the Constituent Assembly who advocated for women's rights is truly the stuff of inspiration – and through it all – she never conformed to rules.

Her life was a true example of recognizing one's privilege and using it for those bereft of it.

As her granddaughter Subhashini Ali proudly said, *'I have never seen a woman like her – so independent and fierce.'*

2

ANNIE MASCARENE

Arrested numerous times for speaking the truth, having her home pelted with stones for pointing fingers at corruption, and toppling an entire Cabinet for fighting for justice – this politician was no pushover. Her entire life was a fight against injustice and discrimination. She fought for better jail facilities for women, was vocal about the underrepresentation of women in Parliament and advocated against unjust laws.

Who was this firecracker? She was Annie Mascarene and here's her story.

Growing Up and Going Beyond

It isn't often that twenty-two-year-old young women are invited for tea with a queen. But that was how it was for Annie Mascarene who got the opportunity, in 1924, to have tea with Maharani Sethu Lakshmi Bayi for being a brilliant student. She and some fellow women students were invited for their academic excellence.

What's all the fuss over tea one may ask? The event is significant because Annie was born on the other side of privilege – she had to fight every step of the way.

She was from a marginalized Latin Catholic community in the princely state of Travancore (now part of modern-day Kerala). For years Annie's fisherfolk community remained on the fringes of the cosmopolitan and progressive Travancore society. Gabriel Mascarene, Annie's father, was a low-ranking official in the government of Travancore. Annie, born on 6 June 1902, and her two siblings (a brother and a sister) spent their childhood under financial constraints.

Annie Mascarene's struggle for equality was a lifelong quest. A bright student, Annie secured admission into the Maharaja's College in Thiruvananthapuram, considered the best for higher education in the region. Impressed by the quality of education at the institution, the government of Travancore decided to fund the education of 80 of its 500-odd students. Only the brightest could find a seat at Maharaja's College; therefore, the public held its students and teachers in high esteem. Annie's academic brilliance became her ticket to the coveted institution, making her one of the few women of the time to pursue higher education. But there was a catch. Unlike many other students at the college, Annie's chances of landing a comfortable government job were slim. Up until 1921,

Maharaja's College, Thiruvananthapuram

the Travancore government did not employ women. Being a Latin Christian didn't help her job prospects either. She was part of a deeply communal society where the minorities – such as the Ezhavas (a 'lower caste' Hindu community), Christians and Muslims – were kept away from employment in certain government departments.

Luckily for Annie and the people of Travancore, the 1920s saw a progressive era under Maharani Sethu Lakshmi Bayi, who assumed power in 1924 as Queen Regent on behalf of her nephew. She introduced several social reforms, such as allowing all castes to access hitherto restricted roads and recruitments based on merit. The Maharani also promoted the education of women and girls. As an incentive, women who attended college at the time

Maharani Sethu Lakshmi Bayi

were invited to tea with the Queen at the palace. And that is how Annie had tea with the Maharani!

A Double Degree? Why Not?

Annie rode the wave of change and made full use of the opportunities made available by the Maharani. In 1925, at the age of twenty-three, Annie earned a double MA in history and economics. Immediately after this, she moved to Ceylon (now Sri Lanka) to become a lecturer instead of languishing in the casteist work environment of Travancore, where she would be offered no job. This shows how bold she was. It cannot have been easy to move to another country on her own.

Things took a turn for the better when in 1927, the Maharani who was keen on promoting women's education opened up legal studies to female students. Annie decided to grab the opportunity and returned home. She went back to her alma mater to read law. After graduation, Annie transitioned to teaching law in the same institution.

Annie's political career began soon after, driven by the political rumblings in Travancore. The reign of Sethu Lakshmi Bayi ended in 1931 when her nephew Chithira

Thirunal Balarama Varma assumed power as the Maharaja of Travancore. In 1932, the Maharaja inaugurated some revolutionary reforms intended to smoothen communal rivalries. Ironically, this was the trigger for a lot of political upheavals.

It brought together the marginalized communities of Ezhavas, Christians and Muslims into action, and they formed the All-Travancore Joint Political Congress (ATJPC). Annie too joined the party and became an active member. The ATJPC kept a united front and was critical of the Maharaja's policies and demanded that people from different classes, ranks and groups should have the right to vote. The party grew from strength to strength and soon became the single largest party in the legislature of the 1937 elections.

Stepping Up and Taking Charge

On seeing the success of the ATJPC, a group of prominent leaders from the dominant Nair community proceeded to join the party. Collectively, they formed the Travancore State Congress (TSC) in February 1938, and Annie was one of its founder-leaders. She regularly authored articles in newspapers and made speeches. The main objective of the newly formed TSC was establishing a responsible government based on the right to vote for everyone. Though elections had been conducted and there was representation of citizens, there was no real decision-making authority given to the elected representatives. It was still a monarchy. Travancore was still under the autocratic control of Maharaja Chithira Thirunal and Dewan C.P. Ramaswami Iyer.

The TSC decided to do something about the abuse of power by the Dewan. They presented a memorandum to the Maharaja to sack him on charges of corruption. This memorandum was signed by all the members of the Working Committee of the TSC, including Annie. However, the Dewan viewed the memorandum as a personal insult.

Of Troubles and Consequences

As a crucial voice of the TSC, Annie made several speeches that were critical of the government. Because of this she faced intimidation and harassment, and multiple attempts were made on her life and property. The first attack, in April 1938, was in the form of a warning – the house where she lived with her mother was pelted with stones. In another instance, a constable rammed his bicycle into her. Three weeks later, intruders broke into her house at night and made away with her valuables, not even sparing the clothes and utensils.

Concerned about her mother's safety as well as her own, Annie reported the matter at the Palayam police station. Despite the police inspector's assurance of swift action, no efforts were made to nab the culprits. She then submitted a memorandum to the Maharaja requesting protection. That, too, failed to yield results.

Annie's Voice Gets Stronger

Rather than getting discouraged, Annie, brave as ever, published a pamphlet in May 1938 criticizing the police for its inaction. The then commissioner of police threatened to charge her with defamation if she did not tender an apology, but Annie refused. The commissioner informed the chief secretary that she was a troublemaker spreading harmful ideas against the state. In his regular report to the Maharaja, the Dewan stated that Annie was critical of the government in her writings and speeches and that she was pushing people to not pay taxes and school fees. Subsequently, Annie was booked for sedition and brought to trial. But the court granted her bail.

Looking at the Bigger Picture

Times were changing. The wave of self-rule was sweeping across the nation. In Tranvancore too. The British were becoming increasingly unpopular. The TSC became interested in being a part of a greater India that would fight unitedly against the British rule. In August 1938, in order to suppress the nationalist movement, the Dewan used his special powers to ban the TSC. The government also censored all news to hide the facts about the goings-on in the state. Realizing that it was important for the movement to shed light on the truth for the rest of British India, the TSC sent its leaders to various parts of the country. Annie, who went to Mysore (now Mysuru) and Bombay (now Mumbai), addressed several meetings, and her powerful speeches drew huge crowds as well as the media.

Times She Spent in Jail

Upon her return, Annie was arrested in Chengannur by the Travancore government, at midnight on 13 November 1938. Based on speeches she had delivered earlier in Travancore, Annie was tried for sedition in two separate cases. The sessions judge of Trivandrum sentenced her to eighteen months in jail and fined her Rs. 1,000. This was a large amount back then. She served the sentence. This was Annie's first prison term, but it certainly wasn't her last.

Annie, after her release from jail, in 1942, gave a speech protesting the arrest of Gandhi and other leaders during the Quit India Movement. Once again, she was packed off to prison, this time with a two-year term and a fine of Rs. 500.

Even after her second stint in jail, Annie's work with the TSC continued uninterrupted in its demand for a responsible government in Travancore. Soon, the party aligned itself with the Indian National Congress (INC) and its ideals. This brought on a bit of trouble for Annie again.

Arguing with Gandhi

To learn more about and immerse herself in the freedom struggle outside of Travancore, Annie travelled across western India and spent time in Gandhi's ashram at Wardha, in modern-day Maharashtra, as well as the Sabarmati Ashram in Ahmedabad.

Gandhi scolded Annie for a speech she made in Bombay. He advised her not to get carried away with emotions and keep a check on the words she spoke in a public forum.

Despite the harsh criticism from Gandhi, Annie persevered in her fight for the people of Travancore. She did not care about popularity; her mission was to speak up for marginalized communities. If her speeches bothered leaders, she was not one to tone down her spirit.

To the Jail Once Again...

The protests for a responsible government in Travancore, began to bear fruit and some reforms were announced by the Maharaja on 16 January 1946. But like previous times, it felt like the reforms were superficial and angered the public more. Though everyone was given the right to vote, the head of government would be continued to be appointed by the Maharaja, rather than being elected by the people. Additionally, the reforms cancelled reservations. This was a huge blow to the minority communities. Almost all community-led organizations erupted in protests against the proposed reforms. Over the next couple of months, hundreds of lives were lost in the agitation. On 31 October, the strikes were called off and more than sixty organizations were banned by the state.

A few weeks after the unrest, Annie was arrested again for being a troublemaker. She was promptly sent to Trivandrum's Central Prison on 20 November 1946.

Travancore Becomes a Part of India

In June 1947, the Dewan announced that Travancore would be an independent country once the British left India. The news didn't go down well with the masses. There was even an attempt on the Dewan's life on 25 July, which scared both him and the Maharaja. The Maharaja immediately cabled Viceroy Louis Mountbatten his consent to accede to India. On 19 August 1947, the Dewan resigned his office and, a fortnight after his departure, the Maharaja announced the establishment of a responsible government on the basis of the universal right to vote. Travancore became the first province in India to do so. This was a victory for the people of Travancore.

Annie Gets Elected

After the release of the TSC leaders, including Annie, Travancore's first popular-elected government came to power on 24 March 1948. Annie was amongst the three elected women in an Assembly of 120 representatives; the other two were Accamma Cherian and Devaki Gopidas. Together, these three trailblazers advocated for a variety of issues – colleges for women, expansion of public libraries, improvement of food and agricultural production, and development of the coastal area of the Travancore State. Annie also argued for the security of jobs and good salaries to check corruption among employees of public service.

As freedom fighters who were jailed several times, Annie Mascarene, Accamma Cherian and Devaki Gopidas had experienced horrid conditions in the prisons for women. It moved them to strive for better facilities for female inmates.

More Power to the People

As a representative of the Travancore Assembly, Annie was sworn in as a member of the Constituent Assembly on 29 December 1948, two years after the proceedings for the framing of the Constitution had started. Given her legal expertise, Annie was nominated to the select committee on the Hindu Code Bill. Annie's ideas in the Constituent Assembly came from her time working in the Travancore Legislative Assembly and the TSC. She used what she learned from being an activist and a lawyer. Her experience teaching and studying law at Maharaja's College also helped her immensely.

Annie stressed that a true democracy required giving power to the people: '*I am a believer in the right of the people of the province to elect their representatives independent of any control, supervision and direction of any power on earth.*'

Taking a Solitary Stand!

Annie participated in the proceedings of the Constituent Assembly with total commitment. She also multi-tasked as the minister of health and power in the new Travancore–Cochin government, headed by Chief Minister T.K. Narayana Pillai. She was the first woman minister in the Travancore–Cochin Legislative Assembly after the merger of the two provinces in July 1949.

However, six months later, Annie and two colleagues were forced to resign to make room in the Cabinet. She accused fellow Cabinet member E. John Philipose of corruption, causing a split in the state Congress. The government eventually collapsed, and the entire Cabinet resigned in February 1951. Though Philipose won a defamation case against her, Annie left the Congress and contested the first Lok Sabha election as an independent. She earned respect for her fight against corruption and won by a huge margin of 68,117 votes, receiving 1,16,617 votes in total.

Till date, she holds the record of being the only woman ever to win from the Thiruvananthapuram Lok Sabha constituency in Kerala.

Where Are the Women?

On the first day of parliament in May 1952, Annie drew attention to the handful of women in the House, precisely saying, '*On behalf of those few ladies here, I hope that you will give us sufficient protection and opportunities for expressing our opinion in this House.*' She believed that women had not been given their political due in independent India, quite rightly so. Only around 5 per cent members elected to the House of 489 members were women.

Annie stood tall throughout her life. She was uncompromising in her beliefs and did not shy away from doing what was right, irrespective of the price she paid for it. Despite her exemplary work, she lost the 1957 Lok Sabha election. She came fourth and secured only 18,471 votes, whereas the winner got more than one lakh votes. This earthshattering loss marked the end of her public life as a politician.

Six years later, on 19 July 1963, Annie breathed her last. This bold and uninhibited firebrand leader was buried in the Pattoor Cemetery in Thiruvananthapuram.

PREVENTIVE DETENTION ACT

In 1952, Annie advocated strongly against the Preventive Detention Act in Parliament. This was a colonial law that gave power to the police to arrest anyone on the vague premise that they might commit a crime in the future. Her time in prison had shaped her views on individual freedom. When she pointed out that male speakers solely dominated the discussions in the House, she was met with ridicule, with some members questioning whether there were any female detainees at all.

Bent on being heard, Annie then brought up her own experience in detention. 'If I had known anything in life, if I am familiar with anything in life it is detention, detenus, detention camps, police and lock-up. That is why, Sir, I said that this Act and deliberations on this Act should not be the monopoly of men.'

Despite her strong remarks, no reforms were made.

A leader who fought for a just world, Annie put a high premium on the need for the rule of law and ethics. Harassment and threats to her life could not deter her from her chosen path.

In 2013, the vice-president of India, Hamid Ansari, unveiled a full-sized statue of Annie Mascarene in Vazhuthacaud. The chief minister of Kerala, Oommen

Chandy, paid historical homage to the courageous personality 'in the forefront of the freedom struggle in Travancore'.

Statue of Annie Mascarene, Vazhuthacaud

3

BEGUM QUDSIA AIZAZ RASUL

When Begum Qudsia Aizaz Rasul stepped off the train at the railway station, only to get into a curtained palanquin which her mother-in-law had sent, it was true that the public and the press had snickered.

Here was a woman claiming to have shed the purdah to enter a life of public service. She even had a fatwa against her for this very reason, so why was she seen observing purdah at her husband's ancestral home.

Was the begum two-faced? Changing her stance as per her convenience?

Born into Royalty

To understand Qudsia – her name in Arabic meant 'sacred' and 'pure', is to understand the times she was born into and lived through.

Her father hailed from the royal family of Malerkotla in Punjab and was the chief minister of Patiala state from 1911–13. Many years later, in 1930, he was the Indian delegate to the League of Nations. Mahmuda Sultana, her mother, belonged to the ruling family of Loharu, located in present-day Haryana.

A MALERKOTLA STORY OF COMMUNAL HARMONY

In 1704, a Mughal commander, Wazir Khan, put two minor sons of Guru Gobind Singh to death. The then Nawab of Malerkotla, a distant relative of Wazir Khan, went against his ilk and protested the killings. He had appealed to Aurangzeb, the reigning Mughal emperor, to spare the boys. The Sikh guru later thanked the Nawab for his intervention and blessed his house. More than two centuries later, the Muslim-majority Malerkotla saw little violence during the Partition. Communal amity was maintained even during some of the darkest hours in the country's history.

Right through Qudsia's early years, politics and purdah were a part of her upbringing. Her father, Zulfiqar, was an accomplished politician. He was known to run a progressive household, but he expected the women to follow purdah, a custom that kept women protected and separated from strangers. Her whole life she navigated between tradition and modern ways, trying to find a balance in her life. Her father encouraged Qudsia's education even when the family was issued a fatwa that a convent education was un-Islamic. She received her primary education at home, with Urdu and Persian teachers and an English governess. She started attending school only when she was eleven. She went to Jesus and Mary Convent in Shimla and later attended Queen Mary College in Lahore, a girls only academic institution for the elite. She would attend concerts, host parties and indulge in political discussions. Qudsia was interested in politics and her father made her his secretary. This gave her a unique view of the unfolding of political events and key public figures – all from behind the veil.

It is interesting to note, that Qudsia's birth coincided with the enactment of the Indian Council Act 1909, popularly known as the Minto-Morley Reforms, which introduced elections to provincial and legislative councils based on a limited franchise. This meant that Indians could participate in governance of their own country, by being elected to minor decision-making positions, while the British still had control over them. Also, these reforms saw the genesis of separate electorates, which was based on the premise that only a Muslim could represent Muslims or protect Muslims interests. This divided Indians along religious lines. Qudsia was born into an environment where the national fervour was building and when the British divisive policies were peaking. The Minto-Morley Reforms were a catalyst for Qudsia entering politics. But more on that later.

Imagine a Time in India...

For now, let's imagine a time in India when India's female literacy ratio was 1.05 per cent and having the privilege as a young Muslim girl to attend both school and college – albeit while wearing a burqa.

Imagine a time in India when women of many communities were still expected to be in purdah – and you discard the purdah to step into politics.

Imagine a time in India when the zamindari abolition was underway – and having to take a stand objectively, knowing fully well that the abolition would ultimately ruin your livelihood, as you were married to a taluqdar, a wealthy landlord.

Imagine a time in India when the nationalist fervour was on the rise, as were anxieties amongst the minorities – and you had to choose between staying on in India or moving to Pakistan after the Partition.

And finally, imagine a time in India when women's voices were sidelined, and being the only Muslim woman in the Constituent Assembly with the responsibility of speaking up for the interests of the Muslim community and other minorities.

It was a lot to take on, so early in life, Qudsia decided to pick her battles wisely and change tacks with the times.

From being an observer behind the scenes, in 1927, the tide began to change. An eighteen-year-old Qudsia accompanied her mother to visit Mahatma Gandhi in Shimla. Around that time, Sarojini Naidu wrote to Zulfiqar suggesting he allow his daughter to attend an All-India Women's Conference (AIWC) session in Delhi. The AIWC, founded the same year, aimed at promoting the education of girls and women. The 1928 Delhi session was presided by Sultan Jahan, the begum of Bhopal. She was a respected ruler and a patron of women's rights. Qudsia was said to be influenced by Sultan Jahan to discard the purdah, who strongly believed it came in the way of women's education. But it would take a few more years for Qudsia to come out of purdah.

A Suitable Nawab

In 1929, she married, Nawab Aizaz Rasul, landowning aristocrat from Sandila in the Hardoi district of the United Provinces (now known as Uttar Pradesh). It was an arranged marriage and she got the first peek of the prospective groom from behind a curtain when she was in Lucknow to assist her father with some work. After her marriage, she was called Begum Qudsia Aizaz Rasul.

Her husband, Rasul, a leader from the Awadh region, was part of the 1931 United Provinces Muslim Conference.

Begum Qudsia and Nawab Aizaz Rasul

It was attended by distinguished men from the province who later joined the Muslim League. Adding on to the Minto-Morley Reforms, in 1935, Britain enacted the Government of India Act, a new constitutional scheme that gave Indians more autonomy in governance matters. The Act still retained separate electorates, introduced first in the Minto-Morley Reforms in 1909, and reserved seats for women in legislatures. Her father, Zulfikar was a beneficiary of the Minto-Morley Reforms, having been elected to the Imperial Legislative Council from a reserved seat in Punjab.

To Boycott or Not to Boycott

In 1927, the British announced the appointment of the Simon Commission to review the working of the Government of India Act of 1919 and propose further reforms. The Congress decided to boycott it because it had no Indian representative. This led to the convening of an All-Parties Conference (APC) where a committee was formed for drafting a constitution. The committee was chaired by renowned lawyer and activist Motilal Nehru with his son, Jawaharlal, as secretary. They published the 'Nehru Report' which had many constitutional demands made to the British. The document did not mention separate electorates, indicating an end to the provision.

In Punjab, the decision to boycott the Simon Commission caused a rift in the Muslim League. Zulfiqar was part of the group that welcomed the Commission. When the 'Nehru Report' was published, a group of Muslim League leaders, including Zulfiqar, placed on record their disagreement, especially with regard to the issue of separate electorates. Interestingly, years later, Qudsia took a completely different stand from her father and spoke out against the idea of separate electorates.

Taking the Plunge

The separate electorate was her ticket to enter politics. When elections to the provincial assemblies and councils were announced in 1936, Qudsia and Rasul, both decided to take the plunge into politics and stand for elections.

Rasul contested for the United Provinces Assembly from Hardoi district on the ticket of the newly formed National Agriculturalist Party (NAP), a coalition of Hindu and Muslim landlords along with sections of business capital. Begum Rasul on the other hand, contested as an independent on a seat reserved for Muslims representing Hardoi, Sitapur and Kheri districts in the Legislative Council. And although both won, it was a significant win for Begum Rasul as she won from a general seat and not one reserved for women.

Thus began her tumultuous journey in politics.

You Can't Please Everyone!

Even though she won, Qudsia was in trouble. The religious leaders were not amused by her candidature and issued a fatwa, the second recorded incident in Qudsia's case. They declared that voting for a non-purdah Muslim woman was un-Islamic. The anger amongst the conservatives was not only due to her disregard for purdah but also because a woman had dared to openly compete with men. Qudsia had run a spirited campaign, receiving unwavering support from Rasul. She won the election with a thumping majority. To understand the magnitude: only ten women had won the general seats from across the country.

From Purdah to Politics

As she made inroads into politics, Begum Rasul decided to finally discard purdah. She got her chance when she and her husband moved out of the ancestral home and into a smaller place. She now only maintained purdah when she had to meet her traditional mother-in-law at the ancestral home.

The two-faced Begum as she was called, she was anything but that – she was a pragmatic Begum.

She was truly path breaking and along the way, as it usually happens – angered many. The conservatives were upset, because she was not practising purdah and had the courage to stand for elections from a general seat and end up winning! How cheeky!

Qudsia went on to become the Leader of the Opposition in the United Provinces Council between 1937 and 1940 and also served as the Deputy Speaker. During this tenure, she continued to ruffle feathers. She spoke of birth control and asked for more women police officers – topics that were not considered appropriate for public discussion. She strongly supported women's education and pushed for more funding in the budget. She believed that a country's progress depended on educated women, and blamed widespread illiteracy on the lack of education among them.

Bye-Bye Zamindari System

During her time in the Constituent Assembly, Qudsia played a key role in the heated discussions around ending the zamindari system – a system where big landlords, especially in the United Provinces, held huge power over land and farmers.

WHAT IS ZAMINDARI SYSTEM?

The system recognized the zamindars as landowners who then let out their lands to tenant farmers in return of a share of the produce. The zamindar, in turn, had to pay a fixed sum to the British Government. This led to a lot of exploitation of the peasants.

Qudsia's position was complex. On one hand, she supported giving land rights to farmers, urging landlords to do so willingly before it was taken from them. This was a bold stand, especially since her own husband was a taluqdar.

But she also showed sympathy for the zamindars. She felt many of them had supported India's freedom struggle and now risked being unfairly punished. She feared that suddenly taking away their land without proper compensation or support would leave them in poverty, and could even cause unrest and crime.

Qudsia believed that change was needed – but not in a way that hurt one group too harshly. She asked for fair compensation and a balanced approach.

The Indian press scoffed at her – as she kept changing her ideology and remoulding herself.

Post the provincial elections, both Rasul and Qudsia joined the Muslim League. Rasul became secretary of the United Provinces Muslim League in 1937. The following year, Qudsia was appointed to the newly formed All-India Muslim Women Sub-Committee of the Muslim League. The couple's modern ways of not following purdah and throwing cocktail parties did not sit well with some members of the League. Qudsia was not to be intimidated and deftly questioned the hypocrisy of such complaints.

Choosing Freedom or Swaraj?

Qudsia's association with the Muslim League brought her into conflict with the AIWC, of which she had been an active participant since its inception. In the early years, Qudsia often advocated secular policies. The AIWC reaffirmed its opposition to separate electorates of all kinds. In the 1930s, the AIWC had broadened its agenda and was focused on effectively contributing to the freedom movement. Its policies mirrored the Congress's opinion – which led to alienation amongst several Muslim members. At the 1939 session, an idea of a separate conference for Muslims was mooted. During a session, Muslim women led by Qudsia staged a walkout in protest of AIWC policies. The situation escalated at the 1940 session – Qudsia was then the President of AIWC's Awadh branch – over the use of the word 'swaraj' in a resolution calling for communal unity. Some delegates and Muslim leaders had objected to the word 'swaraj', citing its association with the Congress party. But Qudsia urged members to stop focusing on words. She stressed that the real issue was communal unity – without it, there could be no progress, no freedom or swaraj.

The 1940 session ended with the AIWC reiterating its opposition to separate electorates. Qudsia was one of the lone voices amongst the Muslim activists who supported joint electorates. Unlike separate electorates, where candidates and voters must be from the same community, in the joint electorates, seats are reserved for a particular community but voters from all communities are allowed to vote. Qudsia had been elected to the Legislative Council on a Muslim seat. Without separate electorates, she was going to find it tougher to sail through in an election. Despite that, she aligned with AIWC's majority opinion on the issue. However, eventually, as the political atmosphere got communally charged, she chose to be firmly ensconced in the Muslim League.

Call for a Separate Nation

In March 1940 at Lahore, the Muslim League called the administrative framework as provided in the Government of India Act 1935 'totally unsuited to and unworkable' and 'unacceptable to Muslim India'. This was the clarion call for a separate nation led by Jinnah.

Qudsia did extensive work for the Muslim League, travelling to different cities to strengthen the party organization and election campaigning.

Qudsia's support for the idea of Pakistan was complicated – she knew Jinnah wanted Muslims to stand on their own feet and be economically well-off – but she herself had doubts over the financial viability of a separate nation.

Qudsia understood that if India were divided by religion, Muslims living in the United Provinces would be left in a tough spot. When she shared her worries with Jinnah, he reportedly said that Muslims in minority areas would have to make that sacrifice. After Partition, many big Muslim League leaders moved to Pakistan, including people from her own family. In a 1997 interview, Qudsia remembered how the Urdu newspapers questioned why these leaders left, abandoning the poor Muslims with no one to guide or support them. Even though Qudsia had once supported the idea of Pakistan, she and Rasul chose to stay in India. They felt it was their duty to help and stand by the Muslims who remained.

The scale of the violence and devastation that accompanied the Partition was a clear sign of how badly communal politics had failed. In November 1947, Muslim leaders, including Qudsia, had requested security in the wake of the prevailing situation. In the weeks after Partition, India's leaders shifted focus. After seeing the damage caused, they strongly felt the country must stand by secular values and treat all religions equally.

Despite being a member of the Muslim League, she realized that reservation – be it separate or joint electorate – is divisive. The way forward for India was to be secular.

No Minority Should Feel Left Out

Qudsia was elected to the Constituent Assembly in 1946, when she was secretary of the Muslim League. The only Muslim woman at the Assembly found herself thrust forward as spokesman for the Muslim community. She was a member of the Advisory Committee on Fundamental Rights, Minorities, and Tribal and Excluded Areas. The Committee, headed by Sardar Patel, submitted its report in April 1947 and recommended doing away with separate electorates.

She believed that reservations could do more harm than good by creating a permanent divide between minorities and the majority. Instead of bringing people together, she felt it would keep feelings of separation and division alive, which should be ended completely. Begum Rasul suggested that Muslims should throw themselves entirely upon the good-will of the majority community and pave the way for establishing a secular democratic state.

At the same time, she exhorted the Hindus to make sure that the minorities did not feel left out and to instil feelings of confidence, good-will and security. '*Then only can loyalty accrue, because it is the condition of people's minds that creates loyalty. It is not the asking for it that makes for it,*' she emphasized.

Shree S.N. Mukherjee, Dr B.R. Ambedkar and Begum Qudsia Rasul

Her impassioned appeal in the Assembly was successful in building support for the abolition of the separate electorates, and reservation for minorities.

In 1950, she formally joined the Congress. Subsequently, she was elected to the Rajya Sabha from Uttar Pradesh and went on to serve as a member from 1952 to 1956. Qudsia

ADVOCATE FOR MOTHER TONGUE

Recognizing the need for preserving minority languages and cultures, she moved an amendment that would entitle 'any minority residing in the territory of India or any part thereof having a distinct language and script' to 'primary education imparted to its children through the medium of that language and script'. The amendment was defeated at the time. In her later years, Qudsia wrote to Prime Minister Jawaharlal Nehru advocating for educating children in their mother tongues. The 'fundamental rights' chapter in the Nehru Report (1928) proposed free elementary education with the provision of imparting education to minorities in their own language. This proposal did not become an official policy in independent India. Recently, the New Education Policy (NEP) 2020 has recommended the use of the mother tongue or local language as the medium of instruction for primary classes.

was also the first woman to be nominated to the panel of vice chairmen in the Rajya Sabha, or the Upper House.

In the Rajya Sabha, she underlined the importance of equal status and equality of opportunity for women as given in the Constitution of India.

Leaving Behind a Legacy

More than a decade after her time in the Rajya Sabha, Qudsia was elected to the Uttar Pradesh Legislative Council in 1969. Her career in the state legislature spanned twenty years. Between 1969 and 1971, she was the minister for social welfare and minorities in the state. Qudsia was also instrumental in the promotion of women's hockey

PRESS THAT RETHINK BUTTON (AGAIN)

Though she campaigned against separate electorates at the Constituent Assembly, by the end of the century Begum Rasul felt a need for reviewing the official policy. In a message sent to a convention to discuss the status of Muslims in April 1999, she said, 'As communal feelings have grown and the concept of Hindutva has gained popularity, it is time now to think anew of how to improve the educational and socio-economic conditions of Muslims.'

in India. She was the president of the All-India Women's Hockey Association for two decades.

In 2000, she was awarded the Padma Bhushan for her contribution to social work. She died in 2001 and was buried in Sandila, her husband's hometown. Begum Qudsia Aizaz Rasul was an astute politician. What stood out about her was that she was not bogged down by her ideologies. She evolved according to the political circumstances and changing times. And they were certainly extraordinary times that she lived in – so much happened from the time of her birth to her death. Qudsia was able to harness her environment, shake things up in a conservative era and then go on to become a champion of secular and liberal ideas at a time when bigotry and communal passions ran high.

She seamlessly straddled different worlds, braved criticism and carved for herself a place in public life. The only Muslim woman in the Constituent Assembly, Begum Rasul made her voice count, leaving behind a rich legacy of service and an indelible mark on Indian politics.

4

DAKSHAYANI VELAYUDHAN

Dakshayani's first day at college was a special day. There were press photographers waiting to capture the momentous occasion. This was because she was one of the first Dalit women to go to college in Cochin (now Kochi). Many were there to witness the woman who had made history.

Regardless of the hullaballoo made by newspapers to capture her photograph on that morning, Dakshayani entered the college unnoticed. How did that happen? No, she did not have a separate entrance. She had walked right past everyone and yet no one had recognized her. As stereotypes go, the media had presumed Dakshayani would be unkempt with wild hair, as the Pulaya community she belonged to were stereotypically expected to be. She was wearing regular clothes and looked like everyone else.

And that's exactly what she wanted – that people like her, from Dalit and other marginalized communities, be treated as equals – with the same freedom and liberties as every other Indian.

Named After a Goddess

Dakshayani was born to Kunjan and Maani on 4 July 1912 in Mulavukad, Bolghatty, a small island off the coast of Cochin. She was the fourth child, after two sons and a daughter. Dakshayani, a name for Durga. It was an unusual name in a community that didn't name their children after gods and goddesses. Dakshayani belonged to the Pulaya caste, who were then considered an 'untouchable' caste in the princely states of Cochin and Travancore. They had truly little rights and were mostly agricultural labourers who were not even paid. They were not allowed to wear clean clothes, expected to have matted locks of hair, and they were not allowed to cover their upper bodies. Their children could not attend government schools. The punishment for breaking these rules was usually very severe.

But her parents were path breakers and her name was not the only unusual thing about Dakshayani. Her father was a granite construction worker. Her mother was a daily wager in the fields, who also traded in dried fish. Together they broke many social moulds. They used their ancestral home as a space to educate children of their community. They encouraged their sons to cut off their wild matted

DON'T CROSS MY PATH!

Pulayas were not allowed to draw water from public wells or walk on the same roads as the upper caste people. In fact, to prevent any chance of crossing paths, they had to announce their presence every four or five steps. If this call was answered by an 'upper-caste' person approaching that way, the Pulayas had to clear the path by either hiding in the fields next to the road or taking a detour.

hair and wear shirts. Dakshayani's brothers were the first in their community to do so. They faced a lot of taunts and threats from the upper caste people for this act. They were undeterred. Acts of defiance, grit and determination ran in the family.

Overcoming Tragedies

Things became difficult when tragedy struck the family – Dakshayani's father passed away when she was only three years old. The family's financial condition worsened, and their house was mortgaged.

Putting their personal struggles aside, the family became deeply involved with the reformist wave that had washed ashore in Cochin. Dakshayani's brothers were founding members of the Pulaya Mahajana Sabha (PJS).

THE SEA HAS NO CASTE

The year was 1913 and Dalits were barred from assembling on land owned by the Maharaja, so the Pulayas decided to take the matter offshore. According to Dakshayani, 'Dalits met on country boats tied together in the sea at Bolghatty – the sea did not have a caste.' Through songs and poems, they kept the fight for equality and dignity going.

This was also the time Christian missionary schools had been established, allowing the Pulaya children to access free education. A lot of Dalits converted to Christianity, hoping to leave behind some of the stigma that they suffered as Hindus, due to the hierarchy of the caste system. As Christians, the same people could now draw water from wells and walk uninhibited on public roads.

Eventually, Dakshayani's mother and a few members of her own family converted to Christianity. Dakshayani did not convert and remained a Dalit all her life. Perhaps she did not want a simple escape – she wanted dignity, rights and freedom for herself and her community. Something the so-called upper caste Hindus had denied them. She wanted to fight for all of this as a Dalit.

She started attending St. Mary's School in Mulavukad, Kerala. She was a bright student who often answered questions that others in her class couldn't. When it was time to move to senior school, Dakshayani was enrolled at MLCC High School in Chathyathu. This school was so far that it took a ferry ride and a three-four-hour walk to reach. This shows her determination to get ahead in life.

Further, both she and her younger brother started receiving a stipend from the state government after the fifth grade. This helped improve the family's finances and the children eventually stopped their mother from taking up daily wage jobs. They even got their mortgaged house back.

Dakshayani's brilliance shone right from her school days to her college education. Her college days were remarkable in several aspects. Those were the days when one could see very few women in science. She chose to study B.Sc. Chemistry at Maharaja's College in Cochin. In fact, Dakshayani was one of the first Dalit women to go to college in Cochin. This became a media buzz – but the fizz subsided as soon as she entered college.

Education from a Distance

Inside the college, the reception was not so warm. Discrimination followed her within the classroom, as one of her upper-caste teachers would not show her any of the practical experiments. Instead, she learnt by observing from a distance and ended up with a second-class division in 1935.

Despite the odds, a purposeful Dakshayani completed graduation and applied for the post of a schoolteacher. In

July 1935, she was posted to the government high school in a village in Trichur (now Thrissur) district. The daughter of a granite construction worker and a daily wage labourer had broken her shackles – by her sheer hard work and determination.

Discrimination Continues to Follow

The long shadow of caste inequality tailed Dakshayani in Trichur too. The Ezhavas were the majority caste in the area. While Dakshayani found them to be friendly and welcoming on most fronts, she was forbidden to draw water from their wells.

On her way to work one day, she found herself on the same road as a Nair woman – considered an upper caste. '*All along the road... there were paddy fields on both sides. The Nair woman asked me to make way for her to pass as she was observing unapproachability. I told her directly to her face, if you want to go, you may go down in the field. The field was four [or] five feet below the road level. As I didn't concede to her demand, she had to do as I said,*' she wrote in her book. The Nair woman later remarked that she had to walk on faeces because the fields were used for open defecation. Dakshayani, quite literally, stood her ground.

In the school where she was a science teacher, her caste identity was not easily forgotten. Her students, who were from class 6 to class 10, took time to warm up to her. Once, at a conference for teachers, she noticed that a Nair woman deliberately sat away from her. In response, Dakshayani began boycotting meetings where Pulaya and Ezhava teachers were made to sit separately from other attendees.

Following the Gandhian Way

In her fights against caste discrimination, she found an anchor in Mahatma Gandhi. She credited Gandhi for the mindset change about untouchability amongst upper caste Hindus. She always said that the change of attitude in people towards 'untouchables' was because of the work of one man and that man was Gandhi. Though Dakshayani was an ardent follower of Gandhi and his principles, her job didn't allow her the time for full-fledged participation in the freedom movement. The financial obligation towards her family kept her from giving up her job. She wanted to boycott classes during the Quit India Movement; she couldn't do so due to the restrictions imposed by the school. But she also didn't hide her allegiance to the leader – she made it clear to her students that she was a Gandhian.

She got married to R. Velayudhan (a social worker and Gandhian, who later became a politician), on 6 September 1940, at the Gandhi Sevagram Ashram in Wardha, Maharashtra.

Kasturba Gandhi, freedom fighter and wife of Gandhi, personally wove a white sari with a red border for the bride. The wedding was officiated by a person with leprosy in the presence of Gandhi and Kasturba.

Wedding ceremony of Dakshayani and R. Velayudhan

A FISHY TALE!

The food served at her wedding was vegetarian, something Dakshayani was not used to. In fact, before the wedding, Gandhi observed her discomfort with the 'chapatti and jaggery' that was served in the Ashram kitchens. Amused Gandhi asked her, 'Did you expect fish here?' Dakshayani recalled, 'He added that we could cook non-vegetarian in our own hut.' However, 'cooking with firewood in an *angithi* made of mud was a hassle', so Dakshayani stuck with the Ashram menu.

Dakshayani and Velayudhan

Dakshayani and Velayudhan went on to have five children – four sons and a daughter. Velayudhan was a graduate of C.M.S. College, Kottayam Arts College, Trivandrum,

A family portrait

and the Tata Institute of Social Sciences, Bombay. He had worked at various jobs. In 1945, he worked as an information officer at the Press Information Bureau, Government of India, in Madras. He held the post till 1948. In 1952, he was elected to the Lok Sabha.

Marriage with Velayudhan remarkably reduced the financial burden on Dakshayani's shoulders. Dakshayani could finally involve herself in things she was passionate about, and not worry about paying bills and running the household. She wanted to actively contribute to social reform.

Did you know Velayudhan was uncle to India's first Dalit president, K.R. Narayanan?

Always valuing education, Dakshayani had sent money from her salary to K.R. Narayanan for his studies at the London School of Economics (LSE).

Stepping Into Politics

In 1945, Dakshayani got an opportunity to be nominated for one of the three reserved seats for the Scheduled Castes in the Cochin Legislative Council. As per the rules, government employees could not be nominated for the Council. So, she resigned from her government teaching job to join the Council. Dakshayani, yet again, broke another barrier by becoming the first Dalit woman in the Cochin Legislative Council.

An elated Dakshayani gave her maiden speech at the Council on 2 August 1945 in English, a choice that surprised many. She pointed out that the funds meant for the upliftment of the depressed classes were, firstly, too little, and were, secondly, used by the ministers carelessly and without much thought and consideration of the actual problems faced.

Dakshayani also drew attention to the lack of representation of Depressed Classes in local governance bodies, such as panchayats and municipalities.

Constituent Assembly Beckons

In 1946, thirty-four-year-old Dakshayani was elected to the Constituent Assembly from Malabar in the Madras Presidency. She was one of the youngest members of this august body.

Dakshayani remained committed to highlighting the plight of the Dalits in the Constituent Assembly debates. She delivered her first speech on 19 December 1946, and it expressed hope for a casteless society. She said, '*In the Indian Republic there will be no barriers based on caste or community. The* Harijans *will be safe in a Republican State of the Indian Union. I visualize that the underdogs will be the rulers of the Indian Republic.*'

A Fight to Change Society's Mindset

In a discussion regarding candidates for an upcoming election, Dakshayani was struck by the absence of Dalit representation in the Hindu candidates' list in the Muslim provinces. She stated that Harijans belong to the Hindu community – yet their issues are unique because of the oppression they have faced for centuries – and need proper representation across India.

Dakshayani was happy to see the proposal for the banning of forced labour – i.e., employing a person without a salary or any personal freedom. As a daughter of the Pulaya community, who was traditionally enslaved, she welcomed these changes.

Saying No to Separate Electorates

In the Assembly, she emerged as a bold and independent-minded leader. On many occasions, she stood her ground – even when others held a different, more popular point of view.

Dakshayani was against separate electorates, and she appealed to the Dalit members of the Assembly to not insist on them. She said, '*We should not make ourselves the laughing stock of our future generations by harping on separatism. Communalism, whether Harijan, Christian, Muslim or Sikh, is opposed to nationalism.*'

She took on Dr B.R. Ambedkar and S. Nagappa on this matter. They had proposed an amendment that would have required a reserved seat candidate to secure a minimum proportion of votes from Scheduled Caste voters. Dakshayani argued that this was similar to separate electorates.

She also found a flaw in the amendment. She pointed out that if a reserved caste candidate had to secure a minimum number of votes from his/her community, that would make the number of votes cast by members of the other communities not valid. Her clear and solid arguments worked. The amendment was dropped.

Though she sparred with Dr Ambedkar on this amendment and other issues during her stint in the Constituent Assembly, she considered it to be her honour to have worked with him.

On the Abolition of Untouchability

As someone who came from a community considered to be 'untouchable', Dakshayani always spoke up on the issue and fought for its abolition.

In the debate on the abolition of untouchability (Article 17), Dakshayani asserted that we cannot frame the Constitution of India without a clause relating to untouchability. She put the onus of changing the status quo on the oppressors. She shared an anecdote from her time as a college student when a classmate asked her to contribute to a fund for the abolition of untouchability. Her response to her classmate was, '*You people are responsible for this and therefore it is for you to raise the money, and it is not proper that you should ask me for money.*'

Touché! Team Dakshayani!

A Cold Draft

When the draft Constitution was discussed, Dakshayani criticized it for its lack of originality. She termed it as 'totally foreign to us'. She accused the members of the Assembly of not bringing their best in the Constitution. She strongly felt that the Constitution was a reproduction of the Government of India Act 1935, and said, '*We have not left out even a comma from it.*'

Dakshayani suggested that the draft Constitution should be put through a litmus test as an election issue for the people to vote on. But her unique suggestion was not taken into consideration.

The Dynamic Duo

After the Constitution was adopted on 26 November 1949, the Constituent Assembly came to be known as the Provisional Parliament. New members were added to the body, and it functioned until a new Parliament was elected in the first general elections. Dakshayani's husband was also nominated by the Congress to the Provisional

Parliament. With it, the husband–wife duo became India's first Dalit couple in Parliament.

In the 1952 general elections, Velayudhan got elected to the Lok Sabha. With five growing children, their household expenditure was increasing and managing it all with their meagre income as politicians proved difficult. Politics as a full-time job also left them with little time for their children. It was time to take a hard decision. Dakshayani quit politics and took up a job as a publicity officer at an insurance company. For twenty-one years, she held the same job in New Delhi.

In the 1957 general elections, Velayudhan contested, suffered a great loss, and got only 4.9 per cent of the votes and stood last. As they struggled with the loss of his income, their eldest son helped stabilize the family's economic situation with his earnings as a doctor. A couple of years later, Dakshayani returned to politics. In 1971, she contested the Lok Sabha elections from Adoor as an independent candidate. She secured 3,930 votes and finished fourth. This was her last foray into electoral politics.

Dakshayani and Women's Rights

One may wonder why Dakshayani didn't join the women's organizations of the time, like the other women leaders, such as Ammu Swaminathan and Sarojini Naidu.

According to her daughter, Meera, her mother considered it to be an elitist organization. She was not entirely wrong. Dakshayani's trajectory to the Constituent Assembly was quite different from the rest of the women – she had neither been in the women's movement nor been a part of the mainstream freedom struggle. This could be grounded in the fact that Dakshayani wasn't privileged like the others. Her struggle was hugely different from what others had experienced. She had to fight everyday battles of survival – financially and socially. Despite her desire to join the freedom movement, she couldn't due to the dependency of her family on her government salary, which she would have lost if she participated in the resistance movement. She quit her job only after she was nominated to the Cochin Legislative Council.

However, in the 1970s, she started getting involved in women's rights struggle from a Dalit perspective. In 1977, she joined forces with a few Ambedkarite middle-class women to organize a national conference for Dalit women. The conference saw a great turn out. Over 200 Dalit women participated from different states, with their own stories, poems, speeches and songs. She formed the Mahila Jagriti Parishad, of which she became the president. The organization worked to upskill Dalit women in the slums and provided them with adult literacy.

Final Goodbye

After a brief illness, Dakshayani passed away on 20 July 1978, when she was sixty-six years old. Reflecting on her mother's life, her daughter Meera believed that Dakshayani 'always regretted leaving Kerala'. However, her home state of Kerala did not forget the illustrious daughter who came from oppression and earned her rightful place in the highest law-making body in the country.

To honour her contributions, the Kerala government instituted the annual Dakshayani Velayudhan Award in 2019, to recognize women who contribute to empowering other women in the state.

Dakshayani Velayudhan achieved many firsts in her life – the first Dalit woman to graduate in science in Cochin, the first Dalit woman in the Cochin Legislative Council, and the lone Dalit woman in the Constituent Assembly. She dedicated herself to the upliftment of the Dalit community. Even decades after her death, Dakshayani acts as a vehicle for the upliftment of marginalized communities.

5

DURGABAI DESHMUKH

A man tried to enter an exhibition, but the young girl at the ticket counter flatly said no. When she was chastised for this and asked if she knew who this popular man was, the girl said she certainly did. But rules were rules for all – she replied firmly, *'I knew it was Jawaharlal Nehru but that I was only following my instructions and doing my duty.'* This resolute girl was Durgabai Deshmukh. It goes without saying that Nehru was impressed with her conviction. That same fearless spirit guided her through life, and she remained an extraordinary and inspiring woman to everyone who crossed her path.

Durga was born on 15 July 1909, to a middle-class Brahmin family in Kakinada, in coastal Rajahmundry (currently in Andhra Pradesh). She later came to be known as Durgabai, a name given to her by those who admired her. Her father, B.V.N. Rama Rao, and mother, Krishnavenamma, were social workers. Her father tended to those suffering from the plague and cholera, risking his own life in the process. He even took Durgabai along on several occasions and she observed her father tending to the needy first-hand. She was inspired by her parents' selfless work. She spent her life helping the underprivileged. She remained humble and grounded, connected to the people she served.

Though she adored her dad and imbibed a lot of his qualities, there was one thing she did blame him for – her early marriage. She was married off when she was only eight years old to Subba Rao, a wealthy zamindar. When she was fifteen and considered ready to live with her husband – she flatly refused to do so. She even convinced him to marry someone else.

Even before she was a teenager, she was already busy with social work and had impressed Mahatma Gandhi and Jawaharlal Nehru. Both leaders influenced her greatly and Nehru played a huge role in her political career throughout her life.

On Quitting English

She took Gandhi's call for non-cooperation very seriously. In protest during the Swadeshi Movement, she quit school after completing fifth standard because English was a part of the curriculum from sixth standard onwards. Though it might seem like a strange thing to do – such were the times. The whole country was caught up with the freedom movement. Everyone was protesting in their own way – burning foreign cloth, boycotting British goods, rejecting the English language, quitting government jobs, etc. Hence, she had the wholehearted support of her parents. The whole family decided to wear only handwoven and hand-spun khadi. She even threw all her mill-made clothes into a bonfire, showing her commitment to the cause.

It was many years later that she came back to English, and she learnt it as an adult in order to pursue higher studies.

Durgabai's Unwavering Determination

In this manner, her social activism kicked off on a high note. But Durgabai wanted to do more than just quitting school and burning cloth. On hearing about Gandhi's visit to her town, she wanted to make the most of it and raise awareness of the social evils that women faced. She was always sensitive to the injustices around her, especially towards women. The devadasi system – the practice of dedicating women to a deity and their exploitation by men – perturbed her. Durgabai decided to take up their cause. And this is how she caught the attention of Gandhi quite early on in her activist life.

She first went to the devadasis and discussed Gandhi's work with them to pique their interest in meeting him. The task of organizing the meeting came with various hurdles for Durgabai. While the women were open to the idea of meeting Gandhi, they could not attend a public programme with men. Durgabai had to think on her feet and assured them that she would arrange an exclusive women-only meeting.

The next problem was convincing the local hosts of Gandhi's visit to agree to a women's gathering. Durgabai requested them to spare Gandhiji for at least ten minutes to address a gathering exclusively of women, but they countered with the condition that they would agree only if she collected five thousand rupees for a purse, which they wanted to gift Gandhi.

Durgabai took it as a challenge and raised the sum in just three days with the help of the devadasis. Despite this, the hosts continued to be unhelpful. They refused to find an appropriate venue for the gathering. A determined Durgabai looked for alternatives. After doing some groundwork, Durgabai decided that the girls' school where she studied would be the best option for the gathering and secured her headmaster's approval to hold the meeting.

Now that the venue was decided, Durgabai still struggled to get the hosts to give her the allotted ten minutes with Gandhi. Finally, after repeated pleas, they decided to reserve a mere two minutes of the leader's time for the programme. On the day of the event, according to Durgabai, more than a thousand women were waiting to meet Gandhi. Even before he started speaking, the women were so moved by his presence that they offered all their jewellery and money. The total collection was

25,000 rupees, much more than what the local hosts had asked for.

The two-minute *darshan* ended up stretching to over half an hour. Gandhi emphasized the need for the abolition of the devadasi system, as well as reforms among Muslim women. Durgabai translated Gandhi's speech from Hindustani into Telugu for the audience.

And how old was she when she organized all this? All of twelve years old. Durgabai was truly a born leader.

Unsurprisingly, Gandhi was thoroughly impressed with young Durgabai.

At the main public meeting, which Gandhi had originally come to attend, he told the organizers that he wanted Durga to translate his speech as she had done a splendid job in the earlier meeting.

Durgabai seamlessly translated his speech, impressing him even more. From that day, Durgabai was his translator whenever he visited the South, not only Andhra but also Madras (though she could only speak a smattering of Tamil).

Balika Hindi Pathashala

Two years after Durgabai's first meeting with Gandhi, the Congress decided to hold its annual session in Kakinada. This was also the time when Gandhi was promoting Hindi in South India in a bid to unify India under a common language. It was decided to hold the first Hindi Sahitya

Sammelan along with the Congress session. This gave Durgabai the chance to learn the language systematically. She also learned patriotic songs in Hindi.

In 1922, there was a need for Hindi speakers to coach the women volunteers at the Congress session, the Hindi Sahitya Sammelan, and at a khadi exhibition. Durgabai stepped up to the task. Her parents spared a few rooms in their home, and there, young Durgabai single-handedly taught hundreds of women how to speak Hindi. This was how Durgabai's Balika Hindi Pathasala came to be. Most of the 400 women Durgabai taught were recruited for the Congress session. Unfortunately, Durgabai was rejected because she was only fourteen at the time. Durgabai was slightly disheartened. But she was happy when she was accepted as a volunteer both at the Hindi Sahitya Sammelan and the khadi exhibition. At the exhibit, Durgabai was given the job of a ticket checker, under strict instructions that only those with tickets were to be allowed entry. And this was where she famously denied entry to Jawaharlal Nehru.

And meeting him put her life on a whole new journey.

Even after the Congress session, Durgabai's Balika Hindi Pathasala continued to draw a large number of women. To accommodate them, she shifted the classes to a bigger house donated by a family. The women were also taught to spin the charkha and sing patriotic songs in Hindi.

Many eminent personalities visited the Balika Hindi Pathasala and made offers of help. Instead of financial

SUPPORT AND SELF-RELIANCE

Jamnalal Bajaj, an Indian businessman and politician, was extremely impressed on seeing hundreds of women weaving and singing. He couldn't believe that a young teenager was the founder of the mammoth institution. He even offered Durgabai money to help run the organization, but Durgabai politely declined the generous offer, saying there was no need at the moment, and if ever needed, she would ask him herself. She never did.

contributions, she only accepted books as donations for the libraries. Durgabai held onto this trait throughout her life. She never used her position or fame to enrich herself.

Unfortunately, the school was shut down by the British in the wake of the Civil Disobedience Movement in 1930, along with other educational institutions that promoted nationalism.

But that was not the end of her institute. Balika Hindi Pathasala took a new form as Andhra Mahila Sabha in the city of Madras. Founded in 1937, the organization's main objectives were to empower women by providing adult education and skilling them to generate incomes. A women's hostel for those who came from out of town was also opened. Within ten years, the organization grew from strength to strength. Andhra Mahila Sabha became a full-fledged institution with around 800 members and with various activities such as Hindi classes, classes for admission entrance tests, music and dance, as well as an industrial production unit.

Durgabai's Time in Jail

While participating in the freedom struggle, she was imprisoned thrice between 1930 and 1933. Here, she observed that political prisoners were treated differently depending on their fame and status. The prisons were divided into A, B and C categories. The prominent prisoners had access to a lot of facilities while the C category prisoners – mostly ordinary women – were found languishing. Many did not know of their rights and were uneducated as well. Durgabai found this very distressing, and though she was a Category A prisoner, she demanded to be shifted to Category C. The jail authorities said they could not shift her; the magistrate at the time of trial had decided on this.

So, the next time she was arrested, she specifically asked the judge to make her a Category C prisoner, during her trial. The magistrate hesitated but eventually agreed as Durgabai insisted.

The authorities put her in solitary confinement for almost a year. Her appearance changed drastically, and poor nutrition left her frail. After her release in 1933, at just twenty, her doctor strongly advised her to step away from politics for the sake of her health.

First Things First

She decided to study law to be of service to women convicts who weren't aware of their rights. But before studying law, she had to complete her high school and learn English too. At twenty-four, Durgabai learned the English alphabet with the help of a tutor. Impressed with her learning abilities, her tutor made her appear for the matriculation examination of Banaras Hindu University (BHU) in 1934. After that, she applied for the intermediate examination at BHU. She lived on campus, and politician and education reformist Madan Mohan Malaviya extended his support to her.

Durgabai wanted to major in political science. Unfortunately, Malaviya was conservative in his beliefs and was against women studying a subject he considered the domain of men. But she was determined and didn't let such opinions stop her.

In 1939, she took the special BA Honours examination in Political Science from Andhra University. She secured a first-class division along with a scholarship at the London School of Economics (LSE). In addition, Durgabai got a seat at the prestigious Inner Temple to read law. Unfortunately, the outbreak of World War II came in the way of her plans of studying abroad, so she enrolled at Madras University to complete her LLB degree in 1941. In just four years, she was on the way to becoming one of Madras's leading names in criminal law, thereby proving that some regressive beliefs are meant to be crumbled under the weight of change.

Durgabai and the Constitution

Towards the end of 1946, Durgabai now aged thirty-seven, was elected to the Constituent Assembly. A dutiful Durgabai attended every single sitting of the Constituent Assembly. She was a member of the Steering Committee where Vallabhbhai Patel, freedom fighter and Congress leader, entrusted her with the responsibility of reviewing the amendments proposed by others. Durgabai moved more than 750 amendments, both individually and in collaboration with other members.

TO SIR OR NOT TO SIR?

Durgabai was also the only woman to be included on the Panel of Chairmen of the Provisional Parliament. As the name 'Panel of Chairmen' suggests, the position was held by only men so far. She recounted, 'Once when I was in the chair and a member addressed me "Sir", several members protested and said I should be addressed "Madam Chairman". I, however, said it did not matter how I was addressed.'

In the Constituent Assembly, Durgabai spoke on numerous subjects. Some of her most memorable arguments were about language and age criteria in the Rajya Sabha.

The current eligible age to become a member of the Rajya Sabha is 30 years, but it was originally proposed to be set at 35 years. Durgabai moved an amendment that it should be brought down to thirty. She argued that being older doesn't particularly mean wiser. Eventually, the Drafting Committee accepted Durgabai's amendment and set the eligibility age as thirty.

The debate on Hindi as the national language saw the most impassioned speeches from all speakers, including Durgabai. She called out the authoritarian attitude of the native Hindi speakers in the House and highlighted strong opposition to the imposition of Hindi in southern India. Though she herself was not a native speaker – she had always loved and taught the language to so many others. But she believed forcing the language on people and considering it above other languages was a sure shot of embittering non-Hindi speakers and also losing the support of people like herself.

Defender of Rights! Champion of Justice!

Durgabai stood up for everyone, especially for those who could not speak up for themselves. She wanted to make sure that the Constitution worked for everyone.

Durgabai Deshmukh addressing members in the Planning Commission office, 1953

She supported the article to provide constitutional remedies for fundamental rights. That is, if a person's constitutional rights are violated, they should be able to go to court. On the other hand, Durgabai also believed that rights should not be absolute and was in support of restrictions on fundamental rights. Durgabai stressed that the nation comes above all.

She made an appeal to safeguard children and the youth from exploitation.

The Hindu Code Bill witnessed a lot of opposition from men, many who believed daughters have no right to inherit their father's property. She dismissed critiques claiming that daughters inheriting property went against Indian culture

Durgabai Finds a Partner

Durgabai's work and contribution to the Constituent Assembly had earned her appreciation and admiration from all quarters. She was always known for her sharp mind and forthright manner. In 1951, she criticized the Union Budget presented by the finance minister as being a rich man's budget with no provisions for the poor. The finance minister was Chintaman Dwarakanath Deshmukh, former and the first Indian governor of the Reserve Bank of India. Even after this harsh feedback, to her surprise, she found herself appointed as a member of the Select Committee on the Finance Bill. This is where she began working with Chintaman. What started as criticism turned to respect and friendship for Durgabai. Chintaman, on the other hand, had always admired Durgabai. Working with her, his admiration for her grew. India had just gained independence, and there was work to be done.

In 1952, Durgabai was at a crossroads in her life. She had lost the Lok Sabha elections. She decided to move to Madras to resume her legal practice. But Nehru had other plans for her, and her fate changed again. First, he gave her financial support to carry out relief work in the drought- and famine-hit areas of Rayalaseema (now in

Andhra Pradesh). After that, Nehru sent her on a goodwill delegation to China in 1952, which was led by politician and diplomat Vijaya Lakshmi Pandit.

When Durgabai returned, she learned that she was about to be appointed as the governor of Madhya Pradesh. Her appointment letter only needed the prime minister's signature. But Chintaman suggested to Nehru that her skills would be better used in the Planning Commission, managing social services. Nehru agreed and, in June 1952, Durgabai joined the commission, working alongside Chintaman, Nehru and three others.

Civil wedding ceremony of Durgabai and Chintaman Deshmukh

It was during this period that Chintaman and Durgabai became a couple, even though they were poles apart in personality. While Durgabai was blunt and outspoken, Chintaman was suave and westernized. But their relationship was built on a foundation of patience and mutual respect. They were intellectuals in their own right. Chintaman proposed to Durgabai in November 1952, in his garden. The couple had a registered wedding at Durgabai's residence on 22 January 1953. Nehru was one of the witnesses.

A Visionary Couple

In 1952, Durgabai wanted to resign from the Planning Commission and focus on her family life. But like the rest of her plans, this was not to be. In 1954, Nehru asked her to be the first chairperson of the Central Social Welfare Board, an organization that was to provide services to women and children for their empowerment and protection. Durgabai gladly accepted and served in this position for eight years.

Durgabai and her husband had a pact that only one between them would draw a salary. For them, service to their people came before personal wealth. Eventually, the couple moved to Hyderabad in 1967 to focus on social development activities. They travelled across India and the world on invitations from international organizations and governments. Unfortunately, health problems were to follow. In 1976, Durgabai lost her eyesight to chronic diabetes. In the first few months of 1981, Durgabai's health began to deteriorate steadily. In the early hours of the morning on 9 May 1981, at the age of 71, Durgabai died in her husband's arms.

A child bride who learned the English alphabet in her early twenties, Durgabai dedicated her life to the cause of education and upliftment of every Indian citizen. She received national and international awards in recognition of her service. Several universities awarded her honorary doctorates for her work in social welfare. She used her skillset and made government bodies to implement best practices that benefitted millions. Durgabai was a spirited woman who lived life on her own terms without a care about material gains or personal wealth.

For her, nothing came before service to the country.

Chintaman described her best: '*To know her was to love her. Of censure she had no fear. She was fearless. Pride she had none. Her desire to do good to others was altruism incarnate.*'

6

HANSA MEHTA

In 1947, during the drafting of the Universal Declaration of Human Rights (UDHR) at the United Nations Commission on Human Rights (UNCHR), a bold question was raised – when we say, *'all men are born free and equal'*, does that include women? It was Hansa Mehta, the only woman delegate from India and one of just two women on the entire Commission, who stood up and insisted that the wording must change. She argued that official documents should say *'all human beings'*, not *'all men'*, as the latter was outdated and could easily be interpreted to exclude women. Interestingly, the chairperson of the Commission, Eleanor Roosevelt – activist and former First Lady of the United States – felt that *'all men'* should be sufficient. But thanks to Hansa's persistent advocacy, the final document declared that *'all human beings are born free and equal'*, ensuring that women were explicitly included in this historic statement of rights.

This was a historic moment for India and Hansa. To this day, the UDHR remains the foundation of international human rights around the world. It remains a milestone document in the history of human rights and has been translated into over 500 languages. And it has the contribution of a woman from India. But this was not her only achievement – just one of many.

To truly understand Hansa Mehta – a woman who firmly believed that women's rights are human rights, and the two should go hand in hand – let us start at the beginning.

The Beginning of Hansa Mehta

Hansa Mehta was born on 3 July 1897, in Surat, Gujarat, to Harshadagauri and Manubhai Mehta. Her father, Manubhai, was a philosophy professor at Baroda College (now Maharaja Sayajirao University of Baroda); he later became the Dewan of the state of Baroda under its progressive ruler, Maharaja Sayajirao Gaekwad III (r. 1875–1939).

During Sayajirao's reign, Baroda witnessed major governance and social reforms, including a ban on child marriage and legislation to abolish untouchability. He introduced free and compulsory primary education in the state of Baroda and set up the Baroda College.

Her father was very keen on Hansa getting a formal education. This was quite rare for girls in those days.

Hansa studied philosophy at Baroda College. She was one of the three women enrolled in her batch.

Unlike the progressive atmosphere at home, the college atmosphere was hostile and unfriendly towards the three young women, as the male students and faculty weren't used to having women students around.

During her college years, Hansa and her friends were isolated and forced to keep to themselves. They had to constantly hold back their thoughts and actions. They could neither be assertive nor be themselves.

The men at Baroda College let them down and often took them for granted. Once, they called a strike without consulting or informing the women. On another occasion a student read out patronizing articles on duties of Indian women. Frustrated, she responded with her own speech, voicing the women's perspective. That speech was a success. It gave her confidence to write for the college magazine. She found a way to have her voice heard in an institution that was designed for men alone.

Making New Friends

After completing her undergraduate degree in India, Hansa started a course in journalism at the London School of Economics and Political Science. This was a turning point for her. In London, she became acquainted with Sarojini

Naidu, who was already a seasoned political activist and poet. Naidu had been actively campaigning for women's voting rights in India.

In 1917, Naidu had led a delegation of women that met Edwin Montagu, the secretary of state for India, and Lord Chelmsford, the viceroy. They wanted women to be recognized as 'people', with the right to vote and 'same opportunities of representation' as the men. Despite pushing hard, they met with limited success. The 1919 Government of India Act (based on a report by Montagu and Chelmsford), disqualified women from voting solely because of their gender.

In 1920, parallelly, the women of America were given the right to vote after a long and intense battle, to be treated on an equal footing and given the same rights as men. Unfortunately, feminist leaders knew they still had many more long battles ahead of them in their fight for equality.

It is in this charged political environment that Hansa found a mentor in Naidu, who took her under her wing. In 1920, Hansa accompanied Naidu to the Eighth Conference of the International Woman Suffrage Alliance held in Geneva – an event to discuss the voting rights of women. The exposure made this shy college student become an assertive activist. Newly recruited to the feminist movement, Hansa travelled to the USA to take a closer look at the educational systems there. It was a time of intense learning for her.

Unimpressed at First...

After her tour of the USA, Hansa returned to India. National sentiments were rising, and everyone was talking about Mahatma Gandhi.

Hansa's first meeting with Gandhi was at the Sabarmati Jail, when she accompanied Naidu and a group of women from Bombay. Before this meeting, Hansa had previously seen him from afar on two occasions. At first, she was left unimpressed, but after the second sighting, she was intrigued. Meeting Gandhi in person visibly moved her.

In later years, she maintained a close working relationship with him. Hansa held him in high regard, but unlike others she did not revere him. She believed that one must '*learn and think for oneself... instead of taking shelter behind Gandhiji's words in everything*'.

Breaking Off from Caste Shackles

In 1924, Hansa married Jivraj Mehta, the chief medical officer in Baroda. For a brief period, he was also Gandhi's personal physician. The marriage was regarded as controversial because they belonged to different castes. She said in an interview that her own community wanted to excommunicate her from her caste, '*but then I told them I was going out of the caste myself, as I did not believe in caste.*' Their marriage found support from the king, Sayajirao, who attended their wedding, a very public endorsement of inter-caste marriages. She and her husband had two children.

Hansa Mehta and Jivraj Mehta

Their relationship grew alongside the freedom struggle. They were Gandhi's trusted aides in Bombay and later became members of the Constituent Assembly. Jivraj went on to become the first chief minister of Gujarat in 1960.

Becoming the Voice of Women's Rights

Hansa did not take to the freedom movement immediately and was initially more focused on education and women's rights issues. Her vision was ahead of its times and looked at the root of the problem – child marriage and lack of education. This brought her into conflict with some of the senior leaders of the women's movement. Until then a lot of the Indian feminist movement was seen in small

CAN WOMEN'S RIGHTS BE NON-POLITICAL?

Initially, the AIWC started as an umbrella organization of different women's groups and called itself a non-political entity that focused on education. In 1927, when Britain announced setting up the Simon Commission to study constitutional reforms in India, huge protests broke out around the country. Some members of the AIWC joined the demonstrations.

Many members believed that the AIWC should remain non-political and should not go against the British in India. Others, like Hansa, were in favour of expanding the AIWC mandate. They believed that laws had to be changed to solve women's issues and one had to take it up with the government. The AIWC could not remain apolitical if it wanted change in policy – wanted change in society. While the AIWC retained its non-political character for another decade, Hansa's bold stance made her a name to be reckoned with. Over time, Hansa questioned the methodologies of AIWC. She spoke out that the AIWC was simply mimicking the western women's movement without understanding the problems of Indian women.

pockets and bursts – in progressive cities such as Mumbai, Chennai and Baroda, and many a time seen as a privileged movement. Hansa, on the other hand, established herself as the voice of the young Indian feminists – who were intent on the overhaul of the entire society.

In January 1927, the All-India Women's Conference held its first meeting in Poona (now Pune) where representatives from different women's organizations convened to discuss educational reforms. The AIWC called for the promotion of female education and implored the government to set the age of consent at sixteen. Hansa strongly pushed to declare child marriages as invalid.

Politics and Picketing

In the 1930s, during the Civil Disobedience Movement, Gandhi called women to join the freedom movement. He talked of 'picketing foreign goods and alcohol'. There were apprehensions amongst the women about breaking the law, which would inevitably lead to their arrest. Hansa, for instance, was unwilling to go to prison as she had young children.

Gandhi sent her a message, asking her to campaign against liquor consumption in Bombay. He added, '*India expects every woman to do her duty at this moment in the fight for freedom.*' Gandhi's message inspired Hansa, and she mounted a strong picketing campaign.

Call for Freedom

With the launch of the Civil Disobedience Movement, Hansa eventually resigned from her post in government office and joined the freedom movement. Soon after, she was invited to join the Bombay Provincial Congress Committee. She took to politics like a duck to water. While the government tried to crush the spirit of the historic movement by arresting leaders, Hansa mobilized the masses against imperial rule. She promoted swadeshi goods by organizing *prabhat pheri*s (early morning processions where the participants walk around singing devotional and patriotic songs) around Bombay and picketing shops selling foreign goods. Hansa was an adept organizer.

Under her leadership, the Bombay Congress held large meetings to propagate the message of the Civil Disobedience Movement. On 1 August 1930, she led a huge procession to mark the tenth death anniversary of freedom fighter Bal Gangadhar Tilak. When the police restricted their movement, Hansa and other Congress leaders sat on the road through the night despite heavy rains. The government responded to the defiance by arresting several prominent members of the party. An undeterred Hansa managed to organize another procession within a week's time, with police permission. Her grit and persistence earned her a place in the Congress Working Committee, the highest decision-making body of the party. Her first time attending a working committee meeting in Delhi was eventful.

The meeting was declared unlawful and all its members, barring Kamala Nehru and Hansa, were put behind bars.

Slogans and Railway Toots

Upon her return to Bombay, Hansa, too, was arrested, but not before a show of strength by Congress supporters while she was still at New Delhi railway station. Records say that railway engines were made to hoot non-stop by the authorities to drown out the cries of 'Inquilab Zindabad' by supporters of Kamala and Hansa who were at the station to greet them. After her arrest, Hansa spent three months in prison on the charge of publishing the Congress Bulletin.

In 1932, she was arrested again, but this time with her husband.

Not on a Reserved Seat

In 1936, elections to the provincial assemblies and councils were announced under the Government of India Act 1935. It is notable that Hansa did not want to contest from a seat reserved for women. She was opposed to the principle of reservation of any kind – be it on the basis of caste, minorities or gender.

Congress leaders had been opposing reservations and separate electorates on the premise that it would widen the gulf among the Hindus, and also between Hindus and

HANSA ON RESERVATION

'We have never asked for privileges. The women's organization to which I have the honour to belong has never asked for reserved seats, for quotas or for separate electorates. What we have asked for is social justice, economic justice, and political justice.'

Muslims. Yet, the British continued to bring out policies such as the Communal Award that ensured separate electorates for minorities and Depressed Classes. Gandhi had opposed this with a fast unto death. He broke his fast with the signing of the Poona Act, which replaced separate electorates with joint electorates. Hansa was a signatory on the pact.

A day after signing the Poona Pact, a conference of Hindu leaders constituted a Harijan Sevak Sangh, which sought to abolish untouchability and work towards opening public spaces and temples to the marginalized communities. Hansa served as the vice-president of the Sangh.

It was in this charged environment against reservations and reforms in the Hindu community, that Hansa successfully contested the 1936 elections. She was appointed a parliamentary secretary for education and health. Hansa worked on some far-reaching reforms that the government initiated.

World War II Breaks Out

However, in September 1939, the Congress was not happy with Britain's decision to make India a part of World War II. The following year, Congress launched the individual Satyagraha. Under the individual Satyagraha plan, Congress workers would go to the people and preach against the war. Hansa was one such satyagrahi and was imprisoned for five months. This was the third time she had been arrested.

While the war raged on, Britain continued to make empty promises to India. The Congress launched the Quit India Movement in 1942. Hansa helped form the prisoner's relief committee to raise funds to aid the families of those arrested.

By 1945, the victory of the Allied Forces was inevitable, and Indian independence was finally on the horizon. Women activists were hopeful that their aspirations of equality were going to be realized in an independent India.

Hansa presided over the annual conference of AIWC in December 1945 where she presented AIWC's Indian Woman's Charter of Rights and Duties. She demanded equal rights in all spheres – education, marriage, right to property, and economic opportunities. Hansa also broached a subject that remains unresolved to this day – the issue of unpaid household work. Hansa passionately voiced, '*It is the work of the housewife. She works from early morning till late at night... It is time that the importance of this work was recognized.*'

Hansa was elected to the Constituent Assembly from Bombay on a Congress ticket in 1946.

In presenting the 'Charter of Rights and Duties' of women, life had come full circle for Hansa since her college days when an errant male classmate thought he could decide the duties of Indian women.

Presenting the First National Flag

On the eve of Independence, 14 August 1947, Hansa presented to the Constituent Assembly the national flag 'on behalf of the women of India'. In her short speech, she said, '*It is in the fitness of things that this first flag that will fly over this august House should be a gift from the women of India. We have donned the saffron colour, we have fought, suffered and sacrificed in the cause of our country's freedom...*'

Role in United Nations

World War II was over. There was so much loss and devastation. The mood worldwide was to prevent any further wars. An international organization for world peace was thought to be the best solution and, in 1945, the United Nations (UN) came into being. India's delegate to the United Nations Commission on Human Rights was

Hansa Mehta and Eleanor Roosevelt

Hansa Mehta. It is to be noted that she was not the first choice, but looking back on history she was definitely the right choice.

Hansa sat on the Sub-Commission on the Status of Women and shared with the delegates the Indian Woman's Charter of Rights and Duties prepared by the AIWC. Impressed with the document, the UN Sub-Commission adopted verbatim the first three paragraphs of its preamble.

When the UNHRC discussed the draft of the UDHR, Hansa made history. She objected to the use of gendered words such as 'all men' and 'brothers' because she felt they might be interpreted to exclude women and were out of date. Chairperson Roosevelt disagreed saying 'all men' was used in the general sense and implied human beings. In the final session, Hansa's suggestions for gender-neutral terminology were accepted. Hansa had done a stellar job in promoting liberal ideas based on justice and equality.

Balancing Religion and Reform

During this time, Hansa was also a member of a Constituent Assembly Sub-Committee on fundamental rights, alongside Rajkumari Amrit Kaur. The Sub-Committee brought up several key issues Hansa had advocated for during her activism days. In its report, the Sub-Committee suggested an expansive right to religion.

Hansa and Kaur disagreed with the broad scope of the right to religion. They were concerned that this might come in the way of social reforms. They put forth to B.N. Rau, the Assembly's Constitutional Advisor, that in the name of religion several regressive practices were followed, such as child marriage, dedication of girls to temples and polygamy. They were anxious that there being no clause in the fundamental rights would make it difficult to wipe out these evils. Eventually, their opposition paved the way for a watered-down right to religion and empowered governments to restrict the right when enacting laws for social welfare.

Uniform Civil Code

Hansa brought up the issue of the need for a Uniform Civil Code during the Constituent Assembly debates. She highlighted that there were 'too many personal laws' that were dividing the country.

Hansa supported removing barriers to inter-religious marriages. She pointed out how inter-religious couples had to renounce religion to solemnize a marriage under the Special Marriage Act 1872. This Act was replaced in 1954 with a legislation that allowed marriages without the parties giving up their religion.

DRAWING THE LINE FOR WOMEN'S RIGHTS

The Constitutional Committee's push to define and enshrine the rights of women had irked a few male members. At the time, Rohini Kumar Chaudhuri from Assam called for 'protection against women'. Hansa silenced Chaudhuri by saying, 'The world would have thought very little of the men if they had asked for protection against women in this Constitution; I am very happy to see that the Constitution does not include that provision. Otherwise, men would have had to hide their faces before the world.'

Hansa continued to actively denounce the practice of purdah and was against providing any special privileges to minorities, other than those guaranteed under the fundamental rights.

Hansa carried forward the demands of the AIWC through her role in the Constituent Assembly. She kept underlining the abysmal status of women in the country, '*The average woman in this country has suffered now for centuries from inequalities heaped upon her by laws, customs and practices of people who have fallen from the heights of that civilization of which we are all so proud.*' She also emphasized the need for equality if India were to truly progress.

Working in Independent India

Post-Independence, Hansa continued to stay busy with women's rights and education reforms. In 1949, Hansa was appointed the vice-chancellor of Maharaja Sayajirao University of Baroda, which she had attended many years ago and where her father had taught. Under her leadership, the university gained a great reputation in both sciences and humanities.

Between 1958 and 1960, Hansa served on the executive board of the United Nations Educational, Scientific and Cultural Organization (UNESCO). She headed a committee on women's education that recommended adopting a co-educational policy at the primary school level. She also suggested doing away with the prevalent norm of separate curriculum for boys and girls.

The Indian Education Commission accepted her recommendations. Always interested in literature, she translated many children's classics into Gujarati. She also went on to author multiple children's books such as *Prince of Ayodhya* and *The Adventures of King Vikrama*. In 1959, she was awarded the Padma Bhushan for social work.

Hansa died in 1995, having left an indelible mark on Indian polity and society. Be it the Indian or international political stage, she understood the pulse of the future and played her part in shaping a global order that was founded on equality and justice.

7

KAMALA CHAUDHRI

To defy your family, who were loyal to the British, and become a freedom fighter – one must be truly independent and strong-minded. And that's exactly what Kamala Chaudhri was. She also had a keen understanding of how society works and the unjustness towards women. She expressed herself through short stories – holding up a mirror to society about the problems women face – exposing the quiet struggles of women battling gender discrimination, suffocating stereotypes, widows living in isolation, and women stuck with uncaring husbands and indifferent households.

She also wrote and spoke about the importance of sound mental health – almost eighty years ago – which was not only taboo but also unheard of in the mid-twentieth century. Later, as a member of the Constituent Assembly, her ideas and arguments were shaped by what she had seen and written about – the problems faced by ordinary people.

Early Life and U-turns

Kamala was born on 22 February 1908, in Lucknow. Her father Rai Manmohan Dayal was a loyal deputy collector to the British government. They were financially well-off and had a comfortable life.

In May 1923, at the age of fifteen, Kamala married Dr J.M. Chaudhri, who was from Meerut. The couple had two sons and a daughter. Over time as the freedom struggle progressed, the deputy collector's daughter formed her own views of the British. She opposed her parents and joined the freedom movement. She even succeeded in transforming her husband into a resolute supporter of the idea of Indian independence. Talk about convincing skills!

Grassroots to National Level

In 1930, at the age of twenty-eight, Kamala joined politics. She was secretary of the Mahila Charkha Sangh that followed the Gandhian practice of weaving and spinning yarn – a quiet yet powerful act of defiance, rejecting foreign cloth and reclaiming India's pride, thread by thread. A staunch follower of Mahatma Gandhi, Kamala was devoted to the fight for independence. She joined the Congress during the Civil Disobedience Movement between 1930–31. Her fearless activism came at a price; Kamala went to jail several times. She also rose in the ranks of the Congress – being elected to the City Congress Committee, then District Congress Committee, and the Provincial Congress Committee. She rose from the grassroots to the national level of the party by becoming the senior vice-chairperson at the fifty-fourth All India Congress Committee session held in November 1946.

Words as Weapons

Kamala was passionate about writing fictional stories about the world around her. She completed a Master's degree in Hindi literature from Punjab University. She was keen to use fiction writing to talk about the social issues of the time. She wrote poems and short stories on patriarchy, feminism and even mental health – a subject that became mainstream only in the recent decades.

Even though her achievements and contributions were remarkable, there isn't much public record available about her body of work.

To learn more about her writings look up these short story collections *Unmaad* (1934), *Picnic* (1936) and *Yatra* (1947).

Contributions to the Constituent Assembly

Kamala was elected to the Constituent Assembly from the United Provinces. On 9 December 1946, she signed the registry as a member of the Constituent Assembly. During the Constituent Assembly debates, Kamala was vocal in her support for the Hindu Code Bill, which was a series of laws to reform Hindu personal law. It was put forth to have one single common law for all Hindus. The Bill included a lot of reforms for women, such as rights for daughters to inherit their father's property. She countered passionately those opposed to various parts of the Bill. Praising the Bill and championing women's rights, she said, *'My personal feeling is that this Bill will prove as sort of a panacea for our women community and the progress of our Indian society, and this will go a long way to benefit our womenfolk who are even today being degraded to the lowest ebb.'*

The Hindu Code Bill had a provision to end polygamy. Kamala was incredibly supportive of this. She emphasized the mental trauma faced by women whose husbands took more than one wife. Kamala understood the problems of women, which often tend to get overlooked in laws made from a male perspective.

Read Our Shastras Before Opposing Divorce!

When various members criticized the right to divorce provision in the Bill as a western influence, she was quick to point out that it wasn't true. Kamala's stance on divorce was clear and she addressed their concerns with clear arguments. She urged people who believed that divorce would destroy the structure of society and was against Indian culture to think again. She said that all the conditions laid down for ending a marriage and seeking divorce are laid down in our shastras.

Religion Is Just a Word of Convenience

There were some members in the Assembly who went one step further in their argument against the passing of the Hindu Code Bill. They said the Bill was not only anti-Indian, but it was also anti-Hindu. Kamala didn't agree with the anti-Hinduism colour that the Bill was painted in. She argued that those who oppose this Bill have expressed the opinion that this will prove harmful to our religion. She wondered why anything with a religious colour highly appealed to the sentiments of the people. She reminded people that in the name of religion a murder had been committed.

She was speaking about the death of Mahatma Gandhi who was assassinated on 30 January 1948, by radicals who blamed him for the partition of India and Pakistan.

Foreign Culture? Go Listen to Our Folk Songs

The Hindu Code Bill faced severe opposition on another count – equal inheritance rights for daughters. The provision was dubbed as 'foreign culture'. Kamala did not agree. Kamala based her arguments on Indian literature –

specifically folk songs performed at weddings since time immemorial. She said, '*This sentiment finds ample expression in our folksongs which have existed for the last hundreds of years.*' She expressly stated that it was an injustice to deny daughters a share of their father's property.

Despite the strong arguments of Kamala and various other women in the Constituent Assembly, the Hindu Code Bill was shelved. It took many years for it to see the light of day yet again. This is something to think about.

Today, according to the Hindu Succession Act (2005), in India, women have equal rights to property, including the right to inherit, own and dispose of property, regardless of marital status.

For each of these revised legal frameworks put in place over the years, the stepping stones had been laid down by Kamala and many other visionary women leaders. The Hindu Code Bill they fought for would benefit Indian women many years later. Their contribution in the making of the Constitution, has come a long way to create a more equal society today.

Life After the Constituent Assembly

Kamala continued to serve as a member of the Provisional Parliament till 1952. After that, she worked for the education of girls in rural areas. She contested the 1962 Lok Sabha elections from Hapur in Uttar Pradesh on a

Congress ticket. She secured 81,999 votes and defeated her nearest opponent with a 28,000-vote margin. In her political career, she focused on making girls and women independent through education and skills like sewing, weaving and pottery. She also helped women get training through village industries so that they could have a source of income.

As seen from her speeches on the Hindu Code Bill, Kamala was an independent-minded person who had a deep understanding of how society functions. In an era when any discussion on mental health was unheard of, she used her pen to draw attention to the subject through fictional stories of women who were oppressed in marriages. Not just that, Kamala used the floor of the highest law-making body of the country to highlight the mental health trauma and angst of women whose husbands took many wives. Her knowledge about Indian literature also enriched the law-making process and brought in an interesting perspective to her arguments.

Remembering Kamala

Kamala died in 1970, leaving behind a great legacy as a champion of women's rights. In memory of her mother, her daughter, Ira, wrote the following heartwarming words to commemorate Kamala, her work and life: *'My heart swells with pride as I remember my mother, Kamala*

Chaudhri, a freedom fighter, poet, and writer... through the stories shared by her about the freedom movement, I developed a keen insight into the tumultuous period enabling me to feel the determination of people to endure and suffer for the sake of freedom'.

8

LEELA ROY

In 1921, a young lady wanted to study at the recently opened University of Dacca (now Dhaka, Bangladesh). But the university only admitted male students. Did the young lady let this deter her? Of course not. She immediately reached out to the authorities, but her request was shot down. *How does one accommodate one woman on a campus of 800 men?* This did not dampen her spirits, but ignited a spark. She reached out to the vice-chancellor and demanded an environment for co-education. Seeing her sincerity, he set up evening classes for Leela and three other young women who also placed similar requests. Having broken this gender barrier, she became the university's first female student to earn a Master's degree.

Let us learn more about this trailblazing revolutionary who never believed in gender stereotypes, worked at the grassroots level for India's freedom, boldly criticized

Gandhi, worked tirelessly during the mayhem of the Partition and dedicated her entire life to public service.

In the Times of Revolution

The story of Leela or Leelabati Nag began on 2 October 1900. She was born in Goalpara, Assam, where her father, Rai Bahadur Girish Chandra Nag, had been posted as a civil servant. Her mother Kunjalata Nag was a homemaker. They originally hailed from Dacca – Leela's maternal grandfather, Prakash Chandra Deb Choudhury, was the first Indian superintendent in the secretariat of Assam in 1891.

Despite having many members in the family with a government job, her father was active in the freedom struggle. Leela grew up aware of the world around her, and her father's engagements sparked her interest early on.

While other girls her age might have dreamt of the usual birthday treats, Leela, on her seventeenth birthday, had other desires. In a letter to her father, she wrote, '*I will consider myself to be very fortunate, if I am able to help even a single person in any capacity. Believe me, this is no vain lecture, this is my heart-felt desire and ideal.*'

Leela was brilliant in academics. She attended Brahmo Girls School in Calcutta (now Kolkata), which was the province's best school for girls at the time. She then transferred to Eden High School, in Dacca, from where she passed matriculation in 1917. After high school, she won a scholarship to pursue a Bachelor's degree in English at Bethune College, Calcutta, the leading higher education institution for women in Bengal (now West Bengal).

An All-Rounder and Independent Thinker

Leela's inner calling to activism came to the fore during her college days, when she emerged as a student leader. Leela was the first woman student union representative of her college. She showed immense leadership skills. Refusing to accept the status quo, Leela stood up against what she felt was wrong. In one such instance, there was a rule for the college students to kneel before the Viceroy Lord Chelmsford's wife and Leela felt this was unnecessary. Her stand was that the wife didn't merit such a stature just by virtue of her husband holding the official position. She organized a protest against this rule.

Apart from activism, Leela excelled in sports, painting and music. She especially loved tennis. In 1921, Leela completed her graduation with flying colours – a gold medal and a cash prize of Rs. 100 for being a top student.

After college, Leela returned to her family in Dacca, eager to continue her studies. Coincidentally, the University of Dacca was established in July 1921. But only for male students. Leela Roy bulldozed her way and would not take no for an answer. She became the university's first female student to earn a Master's degree. Leela soon became a figure of respect among her fellow students, as well as teachers. This was also where she became close friends with Anil Roy, a student at the university. Eventually, he became her life partner and biggest supporter.

While at the university, Leela became actively involved in the movement for voting rights for women. Earlier in 1919, despite the demand for women's voting rights on a national level, the Montagu-Chelmsford reforms by the British made it into a provincial issue. It was up to each province to pass their own laws on whether or not women get to vote. Now women's rights groups had to work locally. The groups in Bengal worked towards garnering the support of the elected members of the Bengal Legislative Council.

Leela became assistant secretary of a group in Dacca called the Nikhil Banga Nari Votadhikar Samiti, started by a journalist named Kumudini Basu. The group held public meetings to tell people why women should get the right to vote. It was only in 1925 that women in Bengal got the right to vote.

Deepali Sangha: A Beacon of Hope

In 1922, she worked in the Flood Relief Committee of North Bengal, an initiative of Subhas Chandra Bose. She formed the Dacca Mahila Committee to raise donations and relief goods for flood survivors. While working on the ground, she realized the massive lack of social and political awareness amongst rural women.

Leela knew that true independence for women meant financial freedom, and that education was the key to achieving it. She also believed that political awareness would give women a stronger voice in society. With this vision, Leela and her friends founded the Deepali Sangha Women's Association in December 1923 to work toward these goals.

They built twelve free primary schools, adult education centres, and handicraft and technical training centres. Amongst these, the most popular was the Nari Siksha Mandir. It admitted women from all walks of life – young girls, married women, widows, as well as older women. Other than education till the matriculation level, the institution also skilled women in sewing, handicraft making, forms of arts and culture, self-defence, history and geography. It also had a residency wing, which provided lodging to women who visited Dacca and had nowhere to stay. With branches all over the city, Deepali Sangha was a beacon of hope for the women of Dacca.

Shoulder to Shoulder

Leela noticed that, even in the fight for freedom, men and women were given quite different roles. She wasn't sure why women were being restricted to picketing foreign shops or weaving khadi. And more importantly, why were women okay with this? Leela wanted Indian women to participate in the freedom movement, shoulder to shoulder as leaders capable of making their own decisions and going beyond the traditional roles as just mothers, sisters and daughters. She wanted to empower women to lead with confidence – to be at the forefront as pioneers, and not just as supporters.

Leela Roy walked the talk. She wanted women to understand the politics of the times, and not just be confined to their homes.

A BIG INFLUENCE

Leela was profoundly influenced by the teachings of Rabindranath Tagore, writer and social reformer. She first met him in 1925, when Deepali Sangha requested to felicitate him. The turnout of the gathering was huge. Thousands gathered to see the polymath who said that he had never seen such a large congregation of women in the continent. Impressed with Leela's skills, Tagore invited her to take charge of the women's wing in Santiniketan in Bengal. Though it was a huge honour for Leela, she declined his offer, as she wanted to continue her work with Deepali Sangha. Tagore respected her passion to fight for women's rights and gave her his blessings to continue her good work.

Within the Fight, Another Fight!

As she dived deeper into the women's movement, the need for drastic change became increasingly clear to her. She felt the need to jolt the system to an awakening, and that meant getting rid of the colonizers first.

Deeply moved by her thoughts and work with Deepali Sangha, her former collegemate, Anil, urged her to join Shree Sangha. Anil and other members of Shree Sangha had often helped out with her organization's social activities in the past. He thought it would be a good idea to have her expertise.

Leela was torn – Shree Sangha pushed for violent revolt, and she wasn't sure if it was the right path. Ultimately, she joined Shree Sangha in 1926.

In 1928, Anil went a step further and proposed that she led Shree Sangha along with him. This didn't go down well with most of the men in the organization. Constant fights broke out between the people for and against her, which ultimately led to the split of Shree Sangha. But it didn't deter Leela from leading Shree Sangha.

Deepali Sangha became the sister organization of Shree Sangha, but each woman was tested strictly before being considered for membership in the latter. And these were no ordinary written exams. They were given tasks in arms and ammunitions. Only those with exceptional performance were given the chance to join Shree Sangha. Those who didn't make it were streamlined into contributing towards the social activities of Deepali Sangha.

The Chittagong Uprising

Throughout this period in Bengal, there were all kinds of protests and revolutions going on side by side. Gandhi announced the Civil Disobedience Movement in 1930. The Dandi March was perhaps the largest organized campaign of the Movement. Gandhi defied the salt making monopoly that the British had and walked to Dandi and made his own salt. This seemingly simple act had ripples across the country, including the province of Bengal. Thousands of people were arrested by the British during the Dandi March in 1930. Revolutionaries decided enough was enough. They decided to strike back against the arrests. They believed this was no time to sit back and be non-violent. On 18 April 1930, more than 60 revolutionaries executed a well-planned raid in the city of Chittagong. They attacked two government armouries and destroyed communication and transportation facilities. In the aftermath, the British were harsh in dealing with revolutionary activities by imprisoning suspects or even killing them. The next four years saw widespread arrests of revolutionaries across Bengal, with 2,167 people placed under detention. Anil was arrested in 1930, and the responsibility of running both Shree Sangha and Deepali Sangha fell upon Leela's shoulders. She rose to the challenge.

Not an Ordinary Women's Magazine!

A year later, in 1931, Leela launched *Jayashree Patrika* – a women's magazine named by Rabindranath Tagore himself. Unlike the usual focus on cooking and housekeeping found in most women's magazines, *Jayashree* broke the mould. Its mission was bold: to ignite patriotism and inspire women across Bengal to serve their country fearlessly. The magazine gave women a powerful platform to share their voices and raise political awareness, it was well ahead of its time.

After the Dandi March and Chittagong Armoury Raid, nationalist sentiments were high and the magazine *Jayashree* was well received. But soon things were about to change for Leela. In December 1931, following the assassination of the Dacca district magistrate by two teenage girls affiliated to Deepali Sangha, Leela and her co-editor, Renuka Sen, were arrested. Following this, both Shree Sangha and Deepali Sangha were banned. Leela was now in prison.

From One Jail to Another

From 1931 to 1937, Leela stayed in several jails. After her initial stay at Dacca prison, Leela was transferred from jail to jail. Many women revolutionaries of Bengal were also in jail around this time. One revolutionary, Helena Dutta, who was with her in Hijli Jail, said she was like an older sister to many: *'Leela Nag came forward to help us in our imprisonment. She guided us through those days with love and affection in such a way that the days became lively, sprightly and sweet.'*

Finally, in 1938, both Anil and Leela were released from jail. They decided to merge Shree Sangha with the Congress based on common socialist ideologies. Impressed by her leadership skills, party president Subhas Chandra Bose nominated Leela to the Women's Sub-Committee of the National Planning Committee. Always a champion for women's rights, she went a step further and proposed the formation of Congress Mahila Sangha. Bose supported it wholeheartedly and worked alongside Leela to inspire women to join the freedom struggle.

However, there was an ideological rift in the Congress that led to Bose's departure from the party in April 1939. Leela and Anil soon followed him to his new party, All India Forward Bloc. A month later, they got married.

Rifle or Hearth: Who Gets to Decide?

In another instance, Leela boldly called out Gandhi's bias in 1940, when he wrote in *Harijan*, an English newspaper, that it was '...degrading that woman should forsake the hearth and shoulder the rifle. It is a reversion to barbarity and the beginning of the end.' Leela's years of work with the Deepali Sangha was to bridge the gap in opportunities available to women and to do away with the very societal gender stereotypes that Gandhi exhibited in his article. Criticizing his patriarchal notion, Leela wrote a rebuttal in *Jayashree*, '*Such artificially constructed divide between the home and the world is absolutely unnecessary – all workplaces outside the house or inside should be equally accessible to both men and women and they should have equal rights in exercising their choice according to their disposition and needs.*' Even after eighty-five years and women breaking barriers in countless fields, debates about their roles continue. Leela's vision was truly decades ahead of its time.

However, in 1942, *Jayashree* was forced to shut down again for its articles against the government. Following

BODY CAN STARVE, NOT THE MIND

While in Alipore Jail, she received a secret message from Bose, 'The day is not far off when you will be free to shine and lead Indian women once again.' Such words of encouragement spurred Leela to sharpen her mind instead of sitting idle in jail. She started reading, like most political prisoners of the time. In a letter to her husband lodged in another jail, she complained about the lack of good reading materials: 'One may eat whatever one gets, but I would rather starve than stuff my mind with something I dislike.'

this, both Leela and Anil were rearrested. This time Leela's stay in jail was gruelling. She fell seriously ill in Dinajpore Jail, but the authorities refused to provide treatment. Her supporters protested the government on the streets, as well as at the Bengal Legislative Assembly. Finally, she was admitted to Calcutta Medical College for treatment and recovery. Leela was then transferred to Alipore Jail.

Tragedy Strikes

Leela was still in jail when Subhas Chandra Bose died in a plane crash in 1945. She was released in 1946, after four years in prison. She never was able to reconcile with the news of Bose's death and, like many others, continued believing that he was still alive. She always thought of Bose as one of the greatest patriots and men of the age.

When she got out of prison, Leela's health had improved. She resumed the publication of *Jayashree* and Forward Bloc, wanting to carry forward the legacy of Bose, her idol and inspiration.

Putting Others Before Herself

In the run-up to India's independence, she was nominated to the Constituent Assembly in 1946. The idea of Partition caused her real distress. In August 1946, Calcutta saw widespread communal riots, known as the 'Great Calcutta Killings'. More than 50,000 people were injured, while around 15,000 died. Leela risked her own life by being on the ground and tried hard to save as many people as possible. According to a survivor's account, *'She [Leela] saved innumerable innocent Muslims at the cost of her own life. It ought to be cited as a unique precedent in the annals of history... I still shudder at the thought of how she rescued me in a car, from the disturbed area of Park Circus.'*

Resigns in Protest

During the Partition, her hometown of Dacca eventually fell in East Pakistan (now Bangladesh). This must have shaken her up. In a meeting with Jawaharlal Nehru, after learning that there would be no alternative to the Partition, she promptly resigned from the Constituent Assembly. Though her stint was short, by resigning she made her stand clear.

Plea Against Partition

Around this time, communal riots reached Noakhali, Bengal, which was to be a part of East Pakistan. Reports of thousands of women being raped and abducted were emerging. So, Leela headed there straight, and dedicated her energy into rescue and rehabilitation of the women. Gandhi also camped there for months to help, and the two became closely associated. Leela still hadn't accepted the

Partition and knocked on all doors in search of a glimmer of hope. In June 1947, she and her husband went to meet Gandhi in Patna, Bihar, to plead against the Partition. Gandhi said, '*My lips are sealed, go and meet Jawaharlal and Sardar Patel. If you are able to organize a movement against Partition, I will lead you.*'

But all their attempts to prevent the division failed and Dacca became a part of Pakistan, where Leela and Anil continued to live. A few months after independence, the Pakistan government issued an arrest warrant for both of them for their activism. With no option left but to protect themselves, the couple abandoned their birthplace and sought refuge in West Bengal in India.

In 1949, Leela kept drawing the government's attention about the seriousness of the refugee crisis. She fought for permanent settlement of the refugees, with land of their own, and to provide a source of income for them, so they didn't have to depend on doles from the government.

Biggest Loss in Her Life

Both Leela and Anil wanted to contest the first general elections of independent India held in 1951–52 to carry forward the ideals of Bose. However, before the idea could concretize, Anil was sadly diagnosed with cancer. He died on 7 January 1952. Leela was heartbroken. She withdrew herself from public life to grieve. But in April 1952, when news of a shortage of food in the Basirhat jurisdiction of West Bengal was reported, Leela sprung to action. She went to survey the area and raised her concerns to the government, which resulted in relief efforts. It was as though public service was in her blood, and she couldn't give up. Around this time, she also started an education centre for girls at her house in Calcutta – it was like life coming full circle.

Dedicated till the Last Breath

She jumped back into politics soon after. In 1952, the Praja Socialist Party (PSP) was formed by Jayaprakash Narayan, socialist and political leader. Leela saw the formation of the PSP as an opportunity to take forward Bose's beliefs. Though Leela was made a national-level member, she preferred to work at the grassroots, for serving the public was in her blood.

But Leela's health was not the same. She suffered two heart attacks. Still, she stayed busy with her work with PSP. She finally quit active politics in mid-1962. She suffered a stroke in 1967, but continued to edit *Jayashree* against the wishes of her friends and family. It was as though she knew she was running out of time and pushed herself to utilize every minute she had left, in an attempt to improve the world. Leela breathed her last on 11 June 1970.

In 2008, Prime Minister Dr Manmohan Singh unveiled a portrait of Leela at the Central Hall of Parliament. Prime Minister Indira Gandhi best summarized her life: '*Srimati Leela Roy was widely respected for the courage and devotion with which she worked for the national cause braving many dangers. She encouraged and stood by a large number of revolutionaries. Her work to organize relief at the time of the Noakhali riots will be long remembered.*'

9

MALATI CHOUDHURY

The year was 1920 and Gandhi had just launched the Non-Cooperation Movement. The nationalist fervour was sweeping far and wide, and anti-British sentiment filled the air. A rebellious 16-year-old girl was to appear for the matriculation exams, but to her, joining the movement seemed much more important in that moment. Always one for action, the passionate teenager ran off to a relative's place in Rangpur (in present-day Bangladesh) in a bid to join the uprising. Her mother tried persuading her to change her mind. She finally relented, came back, and sat for the exams – securing a first-class. But the seed had been sown. She joined the freedom struggle soon after, and in a few years, she became a prominent voice of the movement.

Years later, Mahatma Gandhi nicknamed her 'Toofani' for her exemplary work. Let's dive straight in to learn more about 'Toofani' – a woman whose many nicknames echoed her fearless spirit and her tireless support for those in need.

Born on 26 July 1904, in an aristocratic family in Calcutta, Malati Devi was the youngest of barrister Kumud Nath Sen and Snehalata Sen's four children. Unfortunately, tragedy struck her family when Kumud Nath died. Malati was just three.

Her mother Snehalata was educated and independent, and had grown up in a progressive home. She had a way with words, writing numerous stories and books. She also translated Rabindranath Tagore's works from Bengali to English – the poet and social reformer was a close family friend. She also took up teaching to raise her children. With a strong educational background, Snehalata created an environment that encouraged learning in her household.

Her sons Prodyot and Kula Prasad both went on to become prominent civil servants. Being the youngest, Malati Devi – or Minu – was the pampered child with a rebellious streak.

Doing the Unexpected Was Always Her Thing

Malati did the unexpected when it came to choosing an institution for higher education. Instead of Bethune College, her mother's alma mater and Calcutta's most popular college for women, she chose Visva Bharati, Tagore's university in Santiniketan. However, at the time, the university didn't have provisions for female students. That of course did not deter the spirited teenager who preferred Santiniketan's ashram-like experiential learning environment over government colleges.

Being close family friends with Tagore, Malati directly wrote to him requesting for admission to the institute. With no accommodation for female students, the request made Tagore think of a solution. He decided to offer Malati's mother, Snehalata, a job to become the superintendent of the new girls' hostel to accommodate female students at the university. Her mother accepted the offer and both of them moved to Santiniketan.

This led to the entry of the first girls' batch of 1921–22 at Santiniketan. It was Malati's decision to not take no for

Rabindranath Tagore with students in Santiniketan

an answer that led to generations of women studying in Santiniketan.

At the university, Malati came to her own. She took up music and learned to play various instruments, including the veena and the flute. She also trained in Rabindra sangeet, or Tagore songs, earning praise from Tagore himself for her singing. Malati also immersed herself in the world of art and drama. Tagore's teachings, patriotism and idealism remained a big influence throughout Malati's life.

In 1925, her fifth year in Santiniketan, Malati met a young man, Nabakrushna Choudhury. During his ten-month stay at the university, Nabakrushna fell in love with the vibrant and strong-willed Malati. He hailed from Jagatsinghpur in modern-day Odisha. His mother was not keen on this match. But the wedding did happen in July 1927, with the support of his brother and other family members.

Malati's efforts at fitting into the Choudhury household met with only partial success. Within a few months of marriage, the young couple decided to move to a village called Tarikund, near Cuttack. Malati's lifestyle underwent a sea change here. From soft gossamer-thin saris, she switched to wearing coarse khadi outfits.

Inspired by Gandhi's teachings, the duo even took to farming and planted hybrid seeds of potato, sugarcane and groundnut. They spun and sold khadi, besides running night schools for adults and young boys who were cowherds. They also became parents to a baby girl named Uttara.

Let's Make Salt!

When Gandhi launched the Dandi March against the salt tax on 12 March 1930, volunteers of the Utkal Congress gathered at Inchudi, a coastal village in Balasore district, on a similar exercise.

On April 20, Malati led hundreds of women in making their own salt. They replicated this act of resistance at Srijang, Kujang, Ganjam and other parts of Orissa (now Odisha). The successful salt satyagraha at Inchudi was considered second only to Gandhi's Dandi March. The crackdown on the movement saw the arrests of countless Congress leaders and volunteers. Since a lot of leaders were imprisoned, Malati stepped up by organizing protest meetings in Cuttack, Balasore, Puri and Berhampur (now Brahmapur). At one of these meetings, she set fire to a heap of mill-made clothing items. She was now fully inducted into the resistance movement against the British.

Jail Time Is Family Time

In June 1930, Malati was appointed secretary of Cuttack district Congress. She led volunteers in the picketing of shops selling liquor as well as foreign clothes. Malati was eventually arrested for picketing and sentenced to six months' imprisonment.

At this time Nabakrushna and his brother were already in jail. Her sister-in-law was also arrested in November 1930; and with that, the whole Choudhury family was in jail. With no immediate family to live with, Malati's two-year-old daughter, Uttara, joined her mother in Bhagalpur Jail.

The Civil Disobedience Movement and the arrest of nearly 60,000 people, including Gandhi, garnered worldwide attention in the press. Gandhi was released from jail in January 1931 for negotiations with Lord Irwin, the then viceroy of British India. In March, the Gandhi-Irwin Pact led to the end of the movement and the release of the political prisoners. As a result, Malati and her family too were released from prison in March 1931. Out of jail, Malati jumped back into the cause and continued to strengthen the freedom movement.

On 26 January 1932, Malati was arrested again and sent to Hazaribagh Jail for picketing in Cuttack. By this time, she had given birth again to a son named Binayak, who went to jail with her and Uttara.

~

The goal of socialism is to distribute resources more equitably and create a more just society, often with an emphasis on social welfare.

~

Malati and Nabakrushna often pondered over the question: Can India be truly independent when so many labourers were prey to the zamindari system. They could not buy or own land but worked as landless labourers in others' lands.

They were true socialists – their dedication to depressed and financially weaker sections of society led them to found the Utkal Congress Samyabadi Karmi Sangha in 1933. It became the socialist unit of the Congress party in Orissa. Nabakrushna edited a weekly magazine called *Sarathi* as a mouthpiece of the organization, which bore the slogan, 'Let the Workers Unite' on its cover. They practised what they preached and donated their farm in Tarikund to the organization. Malati even sold her wedding jewellery in order to cover the expenses of the publication.

Around this time, more and more peasant uprisings were taking place across India. The socialists within the Congress fold came together and went to villages to understand the oppression of peasants by landowners, moneylenders and the police. The party workers used the pages of *Sarathi* to describe the plight of farmers. The Utkal Kisan Sangha was formed in 1935, and Malati was appointed the secretary.

Although she had an office, Malti hardly stayed indoors. She built strong bonds with the poorest of farmers. She regularly walked 20–30 km to their villages and often stayed with them to understand their struggles. Wherever she went, she made it a point to sing songs of rebellion, and she even played the flute.

Change Is Welcomed, But the People Want More

In 1936, their province was split into two separate provinces – Bihar and Orissa. Nabakrushna was elected to the Orissa Legislative Assembly in 1937. A lot of reforms were announced including abolition of bonded labour – farmers rejoiced. All the hard work by Malati and Nabakrushna had borne fruit. But there was still work to be done. Dhenkanal was a neighbouring princely state, where the rulers had been given absolute power and there were many oppressive laws against peasants. The common people demanded better governance with accountability and wanted the princely states – known as the Garjat states – to join the new province of Orissa. But the rulers opposed. The clashes and protests led to loss of many lives.

Wherever there was oppression, Malati was at the forefront, fighting against injustice. As part of the resistance movement, she was the only woman leader of the Garjat movement. Malati organized a gathering of 55,000 people on 2 September 1938. However, the outbreak of World War II brought the Garjat resistance to a halt.

Almost four years later, the August 1942 session of the Congress passed the historic Quit India resolution in protest of India's involvement in World War II. Out of the five Congress representatives of Orissa at the session, Malati was the only woman. Soon after the session, most of the leaders were put behind bars. While many leaders did not want to get arrested, to keep the momentum of the movement going, it was decided that it would be a good political move to get Malati arrested as she was a popular figure. Her colleagues wanted her to be arrested in public view to gain the sympathy of the masses.

Malati decided to play her part to perfection. Instead of heading directly to Cuttack, she, along with another leader, took a detour and travelled to Bhubaneswar via Madras to buy time and court arrest according to their plan. On the morning after her arrival in Cuttack, Malati was arrested while on her way to address a meeting. As planned, her arrest evoked strong emotions among the people.

But politics is not a game, and after the attention died down – Malati was still in jail. She spent three years in Cuttack Jail.

I Have a Dream

During her time imprisoned, Malati often thought about the Garjat movement and the children who lost their parents to it and wished to open a school for them. She decided to set it up in a town named Angul, on a piece of land that she owned. After being released from jail, Malati made her plans for the school public and received overwhelming support. In fact, donations poured in from well-wishers across the world because of the goodwill attached to her name. Malati named the school Bajirout Chhatravas, in memory of a twelve-year-old ferry boy who was shot dead when he refused to ferry the British across a river.

The school was formally inaugurated on 11 May 1946 and was open to both girls and boys.

Feels Out of Place

In 1946, Malati became the only woman from Orissa to be nominated to the Constituent Assembly. However, she felt out of place and resigned soon after. Her contribution was more direct.

In the summer of 1946, the restless Muslim League refused to become a part of the interim government.

DARKNESS FOR FIVE DAYS

Muhammad Ali Jinnah asked Muslims to observe 16 August 1946 as Direct Action Day. Members of the Muslim League gave rousing speeches stating that Muslims were ready to resort to unconstitutional methods to get their demands met. Such inflammatory words stirred the masses and lead to riots across Calcutta. Now called the 'Great Calcutta Killing', it was a carnage that lasted five days. 15,000 people died and more than 50,000 were injured. It took intensive military operations to restore peace and only a semblance of normalcy was achieved by 20 August 1946.

The Muslim League did not budge from its demand for Pakistan; the Congress was against a partition on religious lines. There was political unrest brewing.

Exactly seven weeks after the Calcutta massacre, on 10 October 1946, communal riots broke out in the Muslim-dominated district of Noakhali, in Bengal, and the princely state of Tipperah (present-day Tripura). These acts of violence carried on for weeks without any intervention from the government.

As news of the riots spread across British India, Mahatma Gandhi and various other leaders, including Leela Roy, reached Noakhali in Bengal. On hearing of Gandhi's presence at Noakhali, Malati Choudhury wrote to him expressing her wish to be of service there. Afterall, she had years of experience working at the grassroots with the marginalized communities. Gandhi declined her offer saying, '*It will not be right for you or anyone else to come here at present. There is darkness all around which will not be dispelled but only deepen with the arrival of outsiders. The best thing is to remain where you are and do your duty.*'

Heeding Gandhi's advice, Malati went to Delhi instead, as a representative of Orissa in the Constituent Assembly. The Assembly began its first session on 9 December 1946 and in the following days, it debated and discussed the framework of independent India. Malati felt dwarfed as she sat amidst legal luminaries such as Dr B.R. Ambedkar, Durgabai Deshmukh, K.M. Munshi and Gopalaswami Ayyangar. Additionally, she was unhappy with the attempt at writing the Constitution by borrowing from other countries. She felt she was dozing away in the backbenches while the country was aflame. Perhaps she sensed that she would be of more help to the people on the ground than sitting inside the Parliament. Eventually, she resigned from the Assembly. She immediately headed off to the riot-affected areas of Noakhali. Gandhi who didn't want her to come to the riot-affected area was deeply impressed by the pace and efficiency of her rehabilitation work and that's how she got her nickname 'Toofani'.

Steps Away from the Limelight

While Malati pressed ahead with relief and rehabilitation work, Nabakrushna remained busy with his duties as the revenue minister in the provincial Orissa government. In 1948, the duo faced a personal tragedy – Binayak, their only son, passed away. A traumatized Nabakrushna gave up his ministerial position for a quiet life with Malati. But Prime Minister Jawaharlal Nehru wanted Nabakrushna to return to politics. Not one to run away from the call of duty, the distraught Nabakrushna returned in 1950 as Chief Minister of Orissa.

Malati, on the other hand, chose to stay away from the limelight and continued her work in rural areas.

Independence did not change the fate of millions of Indians. There was no miracle. Their lives were still caught in a web of social inequalities, from caste bias to lack of basic resources. It was only the beginning; there was still so much to be done. The Utkal Nava Jeevan Mandal (UNJM) was set up for the cause of tribal welfare, with Malati as the treasurer. Among the UNJM's aims and objectives were the setting up of maternity and child welfare centres, dispensaries, libraries, gymnasiums, co-operative societies and much more.

In 1951, when Malati was made the UNJM secretary and president, she worked in the remotest areas of Orissa. She was anguished at the plight of the tribal people. In 1952, in *Gramasevak*, an Odia magazine, Malati openly criticized the corruption of the government her husband headed. In the article, she commented about the prevalence of unpaid labour and unfair taxation of tribal people. This shows how principled she was, she did not care that her husband was the chief minister. For her, the oppressed and the voiceless always came first.

The One Who Shares Joys and Sorrows

The UNJM was successful in eradicating practices such as *goti* (bonded labour and debt enslavement), *bethi* (forced unpaid labour) and *magana* (forced contribution) in these tribal areas. Her work made Malati a loved leader among the tribespeople. They called her 'Numa' – yet another nickname, meaning the one with whom they shared their sorrows and joys.

Seeking a Quiet Life

Nabakrushna was a capable chief minister, but he could not deal with the politics of power by those who kept eyeing his chair. In 1956, he finally gave up both the chief ministership and membership to Congress. The very next day, Malati and her husband left for Bajirout Chhatravas, in Angul, for a life away from active politics yet again.

Now retired from politics, Malati and Nabakrushna channelled their energy into the running of the school and the UNJM. From convincing landowners to donate their land (Bhoodan and Gramdan Movement), to speaking up against police brutality against innocent villages and working for communal harmony between Assamese and Bengalis, Hindus and Muslims – they worked tirelessly. In addition, during the Bangladesh Liberation War of 1971, when lakhs of refugees flocked to the India–Bangladesh border, Malati joined the Bharat Shantisena, a group started by fellow Gandhians, for relief work.

Vocal Against the Government

In 1975, a state of Emergency was declared by Prime Minister Indira Gandhi which restricted basic freedoms, imposed strict press censorship and imprisoned several political opponents. Both Malati and Nabakrushna were vocal against the proclamation of Emergency and were subsequently imprisoned. While in prison, Nabakrushna suffered a stroke, which left him paralysed. In a massive blow to their work, the government also cancelled all grants to organizations run by them. After the end of the twenty-one-month Emergency, the fight against social injustices brought the Choudhurys back to politics in 1977. On her release, to register her anger democratically, Malati contested against the incumbent chief minister as an independent candidate in 1977 but lost with a very big margin. The result came as a shock to many leaders.

Awards and Recognition Come Her Way

While voters rejected her, various institutions honoured Malati for her immense body of work. She was feted with the National Award for Child Welfare (1987), the Utkal Seva Sammaan (1994) and the Tagore Literacy Award (1995). In 1988, the Jamnalal Bajaj Award was conferred to her too, for her work for the emancipation of women and children.

Unfortunately, a series of personal tragedies struck her in the 1980s, which broke her. She lost two grandsons in 1983, followed by the death of Nabakrushna in 1984. Her daughter Uttara too died in 1988. Though the series of bereavements drained her strength, she continued to be one with strong principles and discipline. In fact, once in the summer of 1997, she declined a meeting with Biju Patnaik, the then chief minister of Orissa, because he was late by an hour.

Following a brief illness, Malati breathed her last in March 1998, at the age of ninety-four. Malati left giant imprints on the history of present-day Odisha. She lived a simple life without any desire for position or power, but gave her absolute best for the welfare of the people.

10

PURNIMA BANERJI

She was one of the most vocal members of the Constituent Assembly. She was the sister of Aruna Asaf Ali – an icon of the Quit India Movement. The Nehru family doted on her, particularly Indira Gandhi. In all the records and references about her – it is clear that she made her long-lasting mark with her independent mind and clear thinking. This fiery leader died young, but her debates and points of view on the making of the Constitution live on and are still relevant after all these years.

The Initial Years

Purnima was born to Upendranath Ganguly and Ambalika Devi in 1911. She was the third of five children in the household. Both Upendranath and Ambalika hailed from influential families with close ties to Rabindranath Tagore. The families shared such a close bond that it was Tagore who gave Purnima her name. She was surrounded by arts and culture as she grew up. There are no exact details about her formal education except that she finished her B.A during her time in Lucknow Jail. The story goes that she requested solitary confinement, which was most unusual, as most prisoners dreaded this. Jailers used solitary confinement as a harsh punishment. But Purnima had insisted, as she wanted to focus on her studies and the common barracks were too noisy. Finally, the jailors relented and moved her to another cell, after Sucheta Kripalani offered to accompany her.

Purnima was a minor when she married Pranab Kumar Banerji, the son of a leading Allahabad-based lawyer, Pyarelal Banerji. The Banerjis were friends with the Nehru family, which brought Purnima close to Vijaya Lakshmi Pandit, Indira Gandhi and the rest of the Nehru family. In fact, the Nehrus had nicknamed her 'Nora'. Purnima was seen very often at Anand Bhawan, the residence of the Nehru family in Allahabad (now Prayagraj).

One Who Reads Is the One Who Thinks

She was an avid reader and often wrote letters to Jawaharlal Nehru and Indira Gandhi about books that she had read or were on her reading list. Such was the closeness between them. Purnima was also an avid birdwatcher and wrote to Nehru about being a 'bit of an expert in bird watching' and Dehradun having 'some of the loveliest birds'.

Purnima was known to be lively and charming. An office-bearer of the All-India Women's Conference, she was pivotal in organizing its activities in Allahabad. At its fourteenth session, AIWC president Begum Hamid Ali was impressed by her work ethic. Showering praises on her, Begum Hamid Ali noted how Purnima was 'moving about like a nymph, radiating joy like the full moon to everyone who may come in contact with her'. Rabindranath Tagore had certainly chosen an appropriate name for her. Purnima was a pillar of support for the freedom fighters who needed help in Allahabad.

Impressed by Socialism

The time spent at Allahabad, then the centre of Congress political activities, and proximity with the Nehru clan brought her close to the freedom movement. It was the period when Jawaharlal Nehru and other leaders, such as Jayaprakash Narayan and Dr Ram Manohar Lohia, were deeply impressed by the Russian experiment of organizing the economy on socialist lines. It also shaped her ideology, as she remained a firm socialist throughout her life. She joined the Congress Socialist party in 1933 when it was formed. The party had a clear agenda that an independent India would guarantee improved labour and economic conditions to everyone and of all occupations.

Before that, Purnima's association with the Congress led her to take part in the Civil Disobedience Movement. It resulted in her first recorded jail term. On 26 January 1932, Purnima, along with Vijaya Lakshmi and several others, were arrested for organizing a public event where the independence pledge was being taken.

After her release, she was recognized for her commitment to the freedom struggle; she soon rose to become secretary of the Allahabad Congress Committee. As secretary, she organized several trade unions and addressed *kisan* meetings in Allahabad to gain their support for the freedom movement.

Purdah *Hatao*!

Purnima was always progressive-minded, especially when it came to doing away with regressive social practices. Among the things she felt deeply against was the practice of purdah. Once during a municipal election, a Congress worker from Allahabad introduced his wife to Purnima. The wife's face was covered in a *chaddar*, a cotton shawl worn over a sari, which was a symbol of respectability and purdah. The sight of the veiled woman irked Purnima, and she ordered that the *chaddar* be taken off. The story goes that the woman never practised purdah again. Purnima was always there to show support and solidarity to women.

Participating in Individual Satyagraha

In 1940, Congress launched individual Satyagraha in response to Britian's decision to make India participate in World War II. As the war was raging, plans to organize a mass movement were replaced with individuals rebelling against colonial rule and advocating against it. Under the individual Satyagraha plan, Congress workers would go to the people and preach against the war. Purnima was among those designated to offer Satyagraha in the United Provinces. She was arrested for the act. Months later, Purnima was arrested once again for participating in the Quit India Movement.

Withered, but Undeterred

The successive jail terms had left Purnima with frail health and in 1943, she fell severely ill. She had been diagnosed with tuberculosis before and the doctors were worried that the ailment had resurfaced. Her marriage also did not work out. But Purnima was always a fighter. Jail sentences, poor health and domestic problems did not stand in Purnima's way of public service.

Purnima's career in the legislature began with the provincial elections of 1946. She served on various committees of the United Provinces Legislative Assembly. The same year, she was elected to the Constituent Assembly. At thirty-five, she was one of its youngest members. She made several contributions to the making of the Constitution.

Exposure to All Religions in Schools

Her first speech in the Assembly was delivered two weeks after India's independence. The members were discussing fundamental rights and religious instructions in schools. Purnima reasoned that exposure to diverse religious thoughts is important for young minds. Her speech came against the backdrop of ghastly violence perpetuated by the Partition of India. Purnima said, *'The State should be perfectly entitled to see that in the formative age of the child, when he is of the school-going age, the religious instruction is controlled and that the syllabus is of such a nature that the child will develop into a healthy citizen of India capable of appreciating each other's point of view.'*

Purnima's amendment gives us a picture of how the constitutional framers conceptualized secularism – how they understood that religion is an important aspect for the common person, but one also needs to respect others' beliefs by being exposed to other religions from an early age.

Secular Aid

Purnima wanted to add the words 'state-aided' after 'state' in one of the clauses that read: 'No minority whether based on religion, community or language shall be discriminated against in regard to the admission into State educational institutions, nor shall any religious instruction be compulsorily imposed on them.' Her argument was that if an institution receives aid from the state, it must adhere to secular norms. Though some members agreed with her, others opposing it said that the clause was included to safeguard minorities. But Purnima had a lot of foresight, because five decades later her speech was referred in a landmark case in the Supreme Court dealing with a minority educational institution. The Court held that when minority institutions take aid, they must comply with certain government regulations. They cannot outright give preference to one community and must observe certain standards of merit.

What a visionary!

The Rights of Detainees

The right to life and liberty was subject to intense discussion in the drafting committee and the Constituent Assembly. Initially, the agreement was on curtailing the right only according to due process of law. It meant that if the government wanted to abridge the right, it had to adhere to established legal principles. Later, the words 'due process of law' were replaced by 'procedure established by law'. The latter allows the state a greater room for restricting freedoms. Some members felt that 'due process' was vague and undemocratic as it gave primacy to judges' opinions over the wish of the elected legislature. There was heavy criticism of the Assembly replacing the due process clause. Several leaders, and the public, had themselves faced unlawful detention and punishment.

The Rowlatt Act of 1919 allowed detention without trial and had been vociferously opposed, eventually leading to the Jallianwala Bagh massacre. By allowing the legislature to curtail the right to life and liberty by 'procedure established by law', the Assembly was perceived to be giving a free pass to future governments to do as they please. Responding to the criticism, an article was drafted that provided protection against unlawful arrests and granted rights to detainees (present Article 22). Purnima put forth that the preventative detention clause (Article 22 of the Constitution of India) must prescribe time limits beyond which a person cannot be detained by the law. She stated that charges against a detainee must be framed within fifteen days and the accused released if trial doesn't start six months after the detention. She even suggested that the detained person, if they are the earning member of their family, must be given maintenance allowance. Perhaps having been unlawfully jailed herself, she was even more passionate towards the cause. Her suggestions were not accepted. Yet her arguments are still relevant. The right of detainees continues to be a contentious issue even today. Governments have enacted legislations that allow detention without trial for long periods. The Supreme Court has held that the accused cannot be 'subjected to unending detention pending trial'. However, in the absence of a clear constitutional guarantee, several accused continue to be detained without a trial.

Should Right to Property be a Fundamental Right?

Purnima remained committed to socialist ideals and this was evident in the debates on the right to property. At that time, the draft constitution included the right to property as a fundamental right. She believed the government should be able to take some property without paying money for it, if it helped bring fairness and justice to people's lives. When land was still owned by a select few zamindars, Purnima opposed making the right to property a fundamental right for all citizens. She wanted a better distribution of economic resources and a chance for every citizen of India to have a fair opportunity to earn their livelihood. Eventually, the right to property as a fundamental right was extinguished in 1978, with the enactment of the 44th Amendment. It continues to be a legal right today.

Is Age Just a Number?

In another intervention, Purnima led discussions to reduce the age of qualification for the state legislative councils from thirty-five to thirty. Her suggestion was accepted by the Assembly and is reflected in Article 173 of the Constitution.

Take Women in Politics Seriously

She argued that since only fifteen members in the Constituent Assembly out of 299 were women, they have to be considered as a minority. She urged her fellow members to take the matter of women's rights with seriousness, as the women like the rest of India were standing upon a new threshold of life. She passionately added: *'As between the purdah-system and the new life which awaits the development of her personality, she is finding a new place in her home and her country and it is difficult enough.'*

Though originally, the Constituent Assembly had fifteen women members, this number fell to eleven following the resignations of Leela Roy and Malati Choudhury, Vijaya Lakshmi's appointment as ambassador to the USSR, and Sarojini Naidu's demise in March 1949. When the Assembly sought to fill the vacant seats, Purnima suggested that only women should replace women. Her suggestion, however, was not implemented.

She Has Her Final Say

Purnima's final speech in the Assembly was made on 24 November 1949, two days before the adoption of the Constitution. Despite some concerns, Purnima was jubilant about the Constitution. She expressed happiness at the fact that the Constitution gave citizens a chance to mould their lives for the better and establish an equitable society. It was important for Purnima that the Constitution not be relegated to a document that gives sanctity to an elected government; but instead, it should provide a framework to deepen democracy. Two months after her final Constituent Assembly speech, she led the chorus of the national anthem after its official adoption.

Purnima died in 1951 following a bout of illness, aged forty. She shone brightly throughout her career in public life. Though not well-known today, Purnima Banerji's contributions are firmly etched on the Indian Constitution.

11
RAJKUMARI AMRIT KAUR

In 1947, Nehru invited this lady to be part of independent India's first Cabinet, where she took charge as minister of health. She was the only woman in the Cabinet. It was a milestone in Indian politics. The message was being sent out to India and the world about women's representation in a newly independent India. She went on to change the face of public health in India, making her one of the most influential women of the 20th century.

Who was she? Let's find out.

A Princess Who Excelled

Imagine being 8 years old when you are packed off to a boarding school in another country. And that's just what happened to Amrit Kaur – the little princess. Her mother, Priscilla Chatterjee, insisted that she join the Sherborne School for Girls in Dorsetshire, England. Her husband, Raja

Sir Harnam Singh, was hesitant, but Priscilla was adamant that her daughter must gain a good education, even if it meant she had to live far, far away. Amrit was unfazed and adjusted quickly. In fact, she did very well for herself. Her performance in academics and her many talents dazzled everyone at Sherborne. She was the head girl, a coveted position at school, and captained the hockey, tennis and lacrosse teams.

Perhaps her father was reluctant because she was the only daughter in a large family of seven sons. Two of their daughters had died early. Amrit was born on 2 February 1889 and was the youngest. Being the only girl and the youngest of the siblings had its advantages, she was pampered by her brothers. She loved riding, trekking and exploring the forests with them.

She spent most of her childhood in Lucknow and Shimla before she was sent to England for studies.

After her schooling, Amrit attended Oxford University. She wanted to pursue medicine; however, her parents did not allow her to do so. Amrit was a determined girl. While other students were devising ways to sneak out of lectures, she sneaked into lectures and learned a lot just by listening to the teachers. This knowledge would prove handy to her later in her public life.

She was truly multi-talented. Amrit was particularly fond of tennis. She is said to have played at Wimbledon and is regarded as one of the finest female tennis players in India. She was fluent in Italian and French, and could play the piano and the violin. During her university days, she travelled extensively across Europe, soaking in the diverse cultures. Around 1909–10, she returned to India. The atmosphere in her country was electric. The buzz in the air was 'self-governance'.

Winds of Change

Amrit's father, Harnam Singh, had gone through a bit of strife early on in his youth. Born in 1851, into the royal family of Kapurthala, Punjab, he studied at a Christian School. In 1872, he left for Jalandhar following a disagreement with his elder brother. Among the many Christian missionaries settled in Jalandhar at the time was Golak Nath Chatterjee, a former Bengali Brahmin who was the first Indian to become a Presbyterian minister, an ordained leader of the Church. In 1874, Harnam Singh, under the influence of Golak Nath, converted to Christianity and married Golak Nath's daughter Priscilla, a year later. Upon conversion, Harnam Singh had to give up his right to the Kapurthala throne. The British were sympathetic to his plight and appointed him manager of Awadh Estates. The family then moved to Kapurthala Palace in Lucknow.

While she was in England, her father's close ties with the British had continued. Her father was knighted in 1898. He was made a member of the Legislative Council of Punjab. In 1907, the British also gave him the title 'Raja', and supported him in starting a separate dynasty.

But the tide was beginning to turn. World War I was on, and change was in the air worldwide. Many of the Indian royalty, including Harnam Singh, wanted greater representation for Indians in the different branches of administration and the armed forces. Harnam Singh appealed to the British for the self-government status.

His nationalist ideas rubbed off on the young and impressionable Amrit. Biggies of the Congress would frequent their residence. Amrit credited senior Congress leader Gopal Krishna Gokhale, who was among Harnam Singh's close friends, for fanning her passionate desire to see India free from foreign domination.

A Quiet Strength

Gokhale gushed to Amrit about Gandhi, who had at the time recently returned from South Africa, calling him a man 'destined to do very great things for India'. Amrit finally met Gandhi when she attended her first Congress event, the 1915 Bombay Congress session. At the session, Gandhi spoke about the plight of Indians in South Africa. His quiet strength and humble conduct won over Amrit's heart and sparked a lifelong bond.

Amrit continued meeting Gandhi post the Bombay session. On a visit to their home in Jalandhar, he asked her to give up all her foreign finery and take to wearing khadi clothes instead.

However, Amrit refused to burn her foreign clothes and found the transition to khadi difficult – the homespun fabric was 'too coarse' for her. While she was keen on immersing herself in the growing freedom movement, the lifestyle changes held her back. Instead, she sought to help by donating money and, on Gandhi's suggestion, took to spinning. Even then, she could not bring herself to wear khadi.

It took a lot of time, but eventually Amrit shifted to living a frugal life in the ashram.

Focus on Women's Rights

Amrit devoted herself to leading India's growing women's rights movement. In 1927, prominent Indian women came together to form the All-India Women's Education and Social Conference (later renamed All India Women's Conference or AIWC) in Pune. AIWC's principal objective then was social and educational reforms. Amrit was a founding member of the conference and, in a short time, she rose to assume the leadership mantle – she was the chairwoman from 1931 to 1932. She took the organization to new heights.

Feminism for All!

She started making waves both nationally and internationally. She was also actively involved with organizing the All-

Asian Women's Conference (AAWC). In 1933, she was part of an AIWC delegation, alongside Ammu Swaminathan, another member of the Constituent Assembly, who made an official submission to the Council of the League of Nations, pointing to the lack of representation of Indian female opinion in the Council. The Rajkumari paved the way for 'non-Western women and their ideas' at these global women's organizations. This is notable as the issues faced by Indian women might not always be the same as what women in other countries face. With all her efforts, Amrit became one of the most recognizable faces of the Indian feminist movement internationally.

The Complicated Issue of Reservation

Along with her AIWC colleagues, Amrit called for the voting rights for women and most importantly, no reservation of seats for women or any communities. They wanted a society of equal rights and no discrimination. But the British were of the impression that without reservation all the communities in India, especially the minorities, would not be adequately represented. There was a lot of debate about who should represent India and who got the right to vote. Under reservation, all voters were eligible to vote, but the candidates belonged to a particular group. However, in separate electorates, both voters and candidates belonged to the same group.

In August 1932, British Prime Minister Ramsay MacDonald announced the Communal Award. The award ensured the continuance of separate electorates for Muslims, Sikhs, Europeans, Anglo-Indians and Indian Christians. The British also announced the extension of separate electorates to the Depressed Classes (communities who faced extreme social discrimination), taking India by storm. This was the complete opposite of what had been recommended in the Nehru Report, a draft constitution, a few years ago. It demanded India's self-rule, basic rights for everyone and a parliamentary system where all adults could vote.

The Communal Award met with fierce opposition from Congress leaders, though members of the Muslim League welcomed it. In September 1932, Gandhi went on a fast demanding its withdrawal. He feared the Award would divide Hindus and weaken the national struggle. Dr B.R. Ambedkar supported the Award, but Gandhi's fast led to new talks. Gandhi ended his fast after the Poona Pact was signed – a deal between leaders of the Depressed Classes and others. The Pact reserved seats for the Depressed Classes within the general electorate.

The storm raised by the Communal Award reached the AIWC. Amrit, who was a staunch supporter of Gandhi, said, '*There is no question as to the reality of unity amongst us women. We want to send our best women and our best men to the councils – once we are divided into sects and communities all will be lost.*'

Gandhi's Influence

While the battles for reservations and women's rights raged on, Gandhi remained a steady rock in Amrit's life and a growing influence. After losing her father in 1930, Amrit settled her family affairs and took up active work with Gandhi. She initially worked to organize a spinner's association in Jalandhar. A few years later, in 1934, she

Mahatma Gandhi and Rajkumari Amrit Kaur

joined him at Sevagram, Maharashtra, where Gandhi had established his base after shifting from Sabarmati in Gujarat. Life in the ashram was a challenge, but this time Amrit was prepared. Amrit served as Gandhi's English language secretary, travelling with him often.

In 1938, Amrit undertook a tour in Gujarat's Kathiawar region, spreading the word against untouchability and impressing upon people the need to adopt khadi. Life had indeed come full circle – the Rajkumari who at one time found khadi too coarse was now propagating khadi and self-sufficiency.

Where Are the Women?

Amrit was equally committed to the Congress, but she did not shy away from expressing disapproval over the party's decisions. Amrit once criticized Jawaharlal Nehru over the absence of women in the Congress Working Committee (CWC), constituted in April 1936. Amrit was keen on taking up the matter officially. After pressure from AIWC, Sarojini Naidu was added as a member. The Congresswomen had been at the forefront of the freedom struggle, many of them had even faced imprisonment. Amrit herself faced jail time. She was first arrested in Bombay for taking part in the Salt Satyagraha in 1930. But when it came to decision-making powers, why were women sidelined?

Amrit was at the forefront of the Quit India Movement too, leading processions in Shimla. She even sustained injuries after the police lathi-charged the protestors in one procession. Amrit was later arrested and kept in solitary confinement for eight weeks. The hardship took a toll on her health and she was placed under house arrest at her residence. Her sufferings were not just physical. While captive, Amrit lost one of her brothers, and to make matters worse, the authorities refused her permission to write to her sister-in-law to offer condolences.

An Ode to Women

The unstoppable women's rights champion chose to write something else instead. Amrit used her time under house arrest to pen a detailed pamphlet on women in India. Titled 'To Women', it called upon women living in towns to take to villages and devote their time to social welfare. A keen advocate for indigenous industries, she urged parents to involve their daughters, as well as sons, in handicrafts.

The future health minister even touched upon the importance of medical aid and education in the pamphlet. She pointed out that many men stood in the way of social reform by using tradition as an excuse, and said they needed education just as much as women to understand and support change. Men, she thought, strongly opposed women for acquiring western clothes, advocated for tradition, but they themselves were influenced by the West in the language they spoke and the clothes they wore. This must change.

Making of India

In 1946, Britain announced the creation of an interim government of India to help India (and Pakistan) transition from British control to independence. Amrit's name was included in the proposed list of ministers but was turned down by the Viceroy, Lord Mountbatten. The Viceroy recommended replacing Amrit with a Hindu member. Her status was soon to change. In 1947, Nehru invited her to be part of independent India's first Cabinet, where she took charge as the Minister of Health. Amrit was the only woman in the Cabinet.

Amrit was elected to the Constituent Assembly from the Central Provinces and Berar. In January 1947, she was nominated to the fifty-member Advisory Committee – Amrit and Hansa Mehta were the only women on the committee, later joined by Begum Qudsia Aizaz Rasul. Amrit was also nominated to the sub-committees on fundamental rights (alongside Mehta) and minorities.

How Does One Write a Constitution?

Indian society was rife with caste, communal and class barriers. Newly independent India had to put up a united front. The Constitution makers were aware about the task before them – to be inclusive, while achieving the progressive goals of justice, liberty and equality. They had their work cut out. The framing of the fundamental rights saw Amrit participate in many debates and make several valid points.

Positive Discrimination

It was clear that the Constitution would guarantee equality between people as a fundamental right. The framers added another clause that expressly prohibited the State from discriminating against any citizen – the present Article 15. For the countless citizens denied entry to public places and access to water, a constitutional promise of equality was a small but powerful step towards dignity. During a discussion on Article 15, Amrit went a step further. She joined other members to highlight the need for positive discrimination. The members agreed there should be a clear rule against discrimination, but also a special clause allowing separate facilities for women and children. This became Article 15(3), which says the State can make special rules for women and children.

Right to Religion Should Not Come in the Way of Social Reforms

One of the fundamental rights in the constitution is the right to religion. During the discussions by the draft committee on the clause, Amrit and her colleague, Hansa Mehta, were of the belief that religion may come in the way of progress and social reforms. They pointed out that in the name of religion practices like, purdah, child marriage, polygamy, unequal laws of inheritance, prevention of inter-caste marriages, and dedication of girls to temples still existed. Their opposition paved the way for a watered-down right to religion that emphasized 'public order, morality, and health' and empowered the government to enact laws for social welfare (Article 25).

Makeover for the Public Health System

Amrit had taken charge of the health ministry at a time when the health infrastructure was in shambles. The challenge before her was to lay the foundation of a robust healthcare network to meet the needs of a large and ever-growing population. She led bold campaigns against malaria, leprosy and other serious diseases.

One of her lasting contributions was piloting the Bill to establish All India Institute of Medical Sciences (AIIMS). One key objective behind setting it up was to attain self-sufficiency in the field of medical education.

However, setting up a world-class institute, required more than legislation. To do so, Amrit leveraged her personal connections with global leaders to secure finances and technology. The effects started showing very early. Between 1950–51 and 1955–56, the number of medical institutions increased by 16 per cent and the number of medical colleges and annual admissions increased by 40

Queen Elizabeth II with Rajkumari Amrit Kaur planting a tree at the new building of AIIMS, New Delhi

per cent. India also witnessed a sharp fall in its death rate (by 14 per cent) and a rise in life expectancy (between 1950 and 1957). People's lives were changing for the better because of improved services.

Amrit was respected across the world and represented India at many international forums. In 1945 and 1946, she was the deputy leader of the United Nations Educational, Scientific and Cultural Organization (UNESCO). She also represented India at the World Health Assembly, as well

LOOK FOR THE NAME

Six kilometres from India's Parliament stands the country's premier medical institution – the All-India Institute of Medical Sciences (AIIMS). Every year, over four million patients and their families pour into the outpatient departments at the hospital's Rajkumari Amrit Kaur Block. For a lifetime consultation charge of a mere ten rupees, these patients get access to some of India's finest doctors and healthcare facilities. Among the 'temples of modern India', AIIMS is one of the country's foremost success stories. AIIMS's establishment is owed to Jawaharlal Nehru's vision and the untiring efforts of India's first health minister, Rajkumari Amrit Kaur, a name that reverberates loudly across the hospital complex and inadequately in history books.

as the International Red Cross Assembly. Amrit's keen interest in sports did not fade away in her later years.

She was the founder and president of the National Sports Club of India, chairperson of the National Institute of Sports and even a founder member of the Rajkumari Sports Coaching Scheme. Her love for tennis saw her helming the All-India Tennis Association. After ten years as health minister, Amrit was dropped from the Cabinet in 1957. However, she continued to be in Parliament as a Rajya Sabha member till her death in 1964.

Born in a royal family, Rajkumari Amrit Kaur renounced a life of luxury and immersed with missionary zeal into the struggle for freedom, and dedicated herself to the upliftment of the oppressed. In the three decades of her public life, she championed the movement for women's rights, served as an aide to Mahatma Gandhi at the most crucial juncture of the freedom movement and oversaw independent India's foundation of public health infrastructure.

Amrit touched countless lives and left her country a far better place than she inherited.

12

RENUKA RAY

During her college days, Renuka was found with a gun in her purse, and her close friend was shocked. He knew she dreamed of a better world and wanted to be a part of the freedom struggle. But was this really the path she wanted to choose in her fight against the British? Renuka was sure that India should be independent and out of the clutches of colonial rule – but how does one achieve this? She was truly confused. She was tempted by revolutionary rebel methods. But in the end, she decided that the best way to be rid of the British 'was the constitutional way'.

A Family of Reformers and Educationists

Renuka was born on 4 January 1904 to Indian Civil Services (ICS) officer Satish Chandra Mukerjee and women's rights activist Charulata Mukerjee in Pabna (in present-day Bangladesh). She was the oldest of four children. Her paternal grandparents had joined the Hindu reform movement, Brahmo Samaj, and her maternal grandfather was highly educated and had been appointed principal of the prestigious Presidency College in Calcutta. Her maternal grandmother was focused on girls' education and founded several schools before becoming the president of the All-India Women's Conference (AIWC). Her household was a hub where all the generation's best minds gathered.

Renuka was still in college when she met Gandhi for the first time. He was in Calcutta to declare the launch of the Non-Cooperation Movement. They met at her relative's house. This meeting changed her life completely. Inspired by Gandhi, she and her friend quit college to join the freedom struggle. Gandhi asked them to go door-to-door and raise awareness and funds for the movement. He also urged the teenagers to spin charkha – the spinning wheel and learn Hindi. These house visits helped her understand how women were treated unfairly in their homes. These women lived in the inner courts of their house and could only be reached after getting consent from male guardians. Many a time they would discreetly tell Renuka to come back when the men were not at home. But they were open to new ideas and donated their jewellery. They too were eager to be a part of the movement. Renuka also helped organize various meetings where Gandhi addressed these women. For many women it was their first time out of purdah, the system which screened most women from strangers and the outside world. She witnessed the potential and power of such gatherings.

To figure out her career plans, Renuka decided to stay in Gandhi's Sabarmati Ashram. For a girl of privilege, living an austere life in the ashram was a different world altogether.

She wanted to continue being at the ashram, but her father and Gandhi decided to send her to London to pursue higher education. Renuka was furious and protested it. Gandhi intervened and explained the importance of getting an education. He convinced her by saying that she would be better equipped to serve her country 'with courage and an independent outlook' after returning to India. In August 1921, despite her reluctance, she sailed to London and enrolled into the London School of Economics and Political Science (LSE).

Love and Violence Don't Go Hand in Hand

While in the UK, Renuka met and fell in love with Satyendra Nath Ray, a student at King's College. He was a year older and provided balance to her impulsive actions. One important instance of Satyen's positive influence on Renuka occurred while the two were still in London. It was he who dissuaded her from taking to violence. Renuka's cousin, who was a member of an underground armed revolutionary group, urged her to join the revolutionaries.

The cousin even lent her a revolver and invited her to join him at the shooting range for target practice. While she mulled over the suggestion of her cousin, Satyen spotted the revolver in her purse and was shocked.

Coincidentally, she also received a letter from Gandhi the very evening the gun was discovered. It was a wake-up call that shaped her future. She soon returned the weapon and refused her cousin's invitation. *'It was lucky that I did so,'* she later wrote in her memoir.

Meanwhile, her education at LSE sharpened her progressive and socialist ideas. In college, she attended lectures of eminent thinkers, including Clement Attlee, who later became the prime minister of the United Kingdom. In her second year, Renuka was elected to the student union. She was the only woman and only Indian in the body. She made the acquaintance of many Indians who would go on to carve a name for themselves in the Indian freedom movement.

Between her classes and political activism, Renuka had little time for anything else. Satyen pushed her to keep up with her studies. When Satyen cleared the Indian Civil Service (ICS) examinations, Renuka became concerned about losing her freedom after marriage to a civil servant who worked for the British in India, but Satyen reassured her that he would not come in her way as a freedom fighter. He kept his word throughout their marriage.

Renuka returned to India in August 1925. Gandhi was in Calcutta at the time. Renuka was embarrassed to reach out to him because she had not informed him about her engagement to Satyen. But on finding out about the two, Gandhi sent for the young couple to visit him. Gandhi informed him that Renuka's first priority will remain service to the country.

Satyen impressed Gandhi by replying that he believed women have as much right as men to work according to their inclination and aptitude. '*No doubt that there will be difficulties at times, but I feel sure that we both have the strength and the courage to overcome them*', Satyen's confidence left Gandhi impressed. With Gandhi's blessings, the couple tied the knot on 26 October 1925. Satyen and Renuka had two children – a son, Rathindra, and a daughter, Ranjana.

Beginning of the Long Walk Towards Progress

Satyen's posting at Bankura district in Bengal – an area with a high tribal population – gave Renuka an opportunity to see and understand for herself what everyday life in rural India was like. Renuka started working for women's welfare in Burdwan (now Bardhaman) and Hooghly. She set up a few mahila samitis that focused on maternity and child welfare, children's education, as well as crèches for working mothers. While advocating for women's rights, she often faced opposition – sometimes even from women themselves.

Renuka came to see how some people were not ready for bold and fast changes in the society. But she continued looking for ways to challenge the status quo when it came to women's rights. She and her friends organized various meetings about birth control and family planning, fighting against media's criticism for talking about such subjects in public.

At the time, the AIWC was disappointed with the Sarda Act, which fixed the marriageable age of girls at fourteen instead of sixteen, which was the demand of women's organizations. In 1934, it asked the government to set up a commission to reform the laws. As the social secretary of the AIWC, she advocated for a uniform civil code – a common law beyond religious laws to remove the legal disabilities of women in terms of their property rights, rights of widows, divorce, guardianship and child marriage. She stated in a report: *'Law can no longer remain static in a dynamic society. It is the duty of the State to adjust and suit the laws of a country to the requirements of the times.'*

Some Progress but Not Enough

The 1930s were exciting times – India was demanding freedom and equality not just from colonial rule, but also from repressive personal laws. Renuka had already written about a need to have a uniform civil code. In 1937, there was some progress – the enactment of the

Hindu Women's Right to Property Act, also known as the Deshmukh Act of 1937; it was a watershed moment in the women's movement. But the Act, though reformist, had flaws. It granted widows the right to the husband's property, but without absolute ownership. The Act also ignored the rights of the daughter in her father's property. Many women's organizations, led by the AIWC, took to the streets to protest the government's tokenistic attitude towards their demands, i.e., reforms were being announced just for the sake of looking progressive.

Renuka and some of her women colleagues turned to Gandhi for advice. He told them that the law is only one element, and that '*...while he was all in favour of equality for women and the law should be altered, what was needed was the transformation of social attitudes.*' He was speaking from the experience of trying to change people's attitudes about caste.

The women's organizations devised a two-fold plan: they would spread awareness and gather public support, and then get the legislature to pass a truly progressive bill. To facilitate this, meetings and processions were held across the country. In Calcutta, Renuka and her team received a tremendous response from the public; both men and women joined in large numbers to support the legal reforms. However, there were also many people who resisted change and opposed the reforms.

Finally, in 1941, the government formed the Hindu Law Committee to review existing laws and appointed

Sir B.N. Rau, a civil servant and jurist, as chairman. The AIWC requested and was granted the right to nominate a member to the Central Legislative Assembly to help in the codification of the new laws. Rau chose Renuka to represent the women's organizations in the Central Legislative Assembly. Initially, Renuka was reluctant to take on the role – she did not want to work with a government that was imprisoning her friends and fellow Indians during the Quit India Movement. However, Rau reminded her of the women's cause and how unfair it would be to the people who had worked hard to get women a seat at the table, and, in February 1943, Renuka became a member of the Central Legislative Assembly.

On 23 March 1943, the Hindu Law Bills on Marriage and Intestate Succession were introduced in the Central Legislative Assembly. The visitors' gallery was packed with women from across the country. To the surprise of the British officials who had nominated her to the legislature, Renuka used this momentous occasion to argue for Indian independence from British rule. She insisted that the Bills being considered were mere 'half measures' and that only a '*free national government... answerable to the people would be able to bring in radical changes by which complete equality could be secured*'. Her empowering speech donned the newspaper headlines the next morning.

The Bill was opposed heavily by some of the members and was then referred to a Select Committee. Renuka took her seat at the table very seriously, but there was only one other woman in the entire Assembly. However, Renuka managed to make her own place in the House and under no circumstance did she lose her spine or voice. Some members of the Assembly assumed she would be a pushover as she was the wife of a civil servant. But she held her ground and her husband supported her.

A Leader in Times of Crisis

Other than political activities, Renuka was deeply involved in humanitarian causes. She rushed to Bengal during the famine in 1943 and arranged a large amount of voluntary donations of food. She also accompanied Gandhi for relief work in the riot-affected areas of Noakhali.

Around the same time, in 1946, Renuka was elected to the Constituent Assembly on Gandhi's insistence that marginalized groups including women should be represented. Yet again, she did justice to her seat at the table by participating in numerous debates, ranging from religious education and the Hindu Code Bill to the Devadasi system and the right to property.

Saying No to Reservation

She also spoke against reservation for women in Assemblies and the Parliament. Ironically, both her nomination to the Central Legislative Assembly and to the Constituent Assembly was on the basis of gender. Renuka

Ray opposed women's reservation because she believed it held women back and underestimated their intelligence and ability. Her belief was grounded in the notion that reservation would limit women's representation to only reserved seats, and they would lose out on being considered for non-reserved seats. In the same vein, Renuka was also against reservation for minorities, and believed it was not self-respecting for them.

The Uniform Civil Code Sees the Light of Day

Given her decades of work to uplift women, Renuka was extremely disappointed by the delays in the passing of the Hindu Code Bill. She and her colleague, Durgabai Deshmukh, took their complaint to Nehru, who assured them it will happen. But it continued to meet with opposition. Finally, in 1952 and 1956, it was broken down into separate Bills, in an attempt to get them passed quickly. Even though Renuka was serving as a minister in West Bengal at the time, she helped the law minister in garnering support for the Bills. She was finally victorious in seeing the laws being passed – this was something that would change the lives of women all across independent India for the better.

Even while Renuka served in the Constituent Assembly, she devoted her time to solving the post-Partition refugee crisis.

She was also a member of India's delegation to the United Nations in 1949.

Renuka contested and lost the 1952 parliamentary elections from Hooghly. Post-election, when she and her friend Durgabai Deshmukh went to New Delhi, they were offered seats in the Upper House, or Rajya Sabha. However, both the women declined the offer. She had after all opposed bicameral legislature (a Lower House and an Upper House) during the making of the constitution and she remained principled. Eventually, she did serve in the West Bengal Cabinet as a minister of rehabilitation. She was elected from Ratua Assembly constituency, in Malda, in a by-election.

MIC DROP!

Apparently, when she accepted the offer, her husband, who was then Chief Secretary of West Bengal, was asked if he would have a problem standing up every time his wife walked into the room. Not missing a beat, Satyen had replied that he 'always stood up when a woman entered the room'.

To the Centre Once Again!

Renuka's time as a minister, from 1952–57 impressed upon her the need for Centre-State cooperation. While she did some outstanding work to rehabilitate the refugees from

East Pakistan, she felt that she could do better with more support from the Centre.

As a result, she decided to enter the Lok Sabha to be in a position where she could influence the Parliament to give due attention to the refugee problem in West Bengal.

Renuka won the 1957 Lok Sabha elections by securing 97,217 votes from Malda. However, she was disappointed by the difference in the functioning of the Constituent Assembly and the Lok Sabha. Everyone seemed to have vested interests. No one seemed very keen on developmental work or figuring out how refugees could be absorbed into the economy of India.

Not one to be cowed down, she made her way. Renuka headed the Study Team on Social Welfare and Welfare of Backward Classes, which later came to be known as the Renuka Ray Committee. It toured the rural areas in the country and recommended pragmatic solutions to improve the lives of tribals.

After the deaths of B.C. Roy and Nehru, Renuka found it hard to survive the internal party politics. During Indira Gandhi's tenure as prime minister, she asked Renuka to come to the Rajya Sabha. Renuka declined and mentioned that she refused it during her father's prime ministership too.

Back to Where She Started

Thus, Renuka went back to Calcutta and focused on social work, an area that she had been dedicated towards since her teenage years. Even while she was occupied with ministerial or parliamentary duties, she had not detached herself from the women's movement. In 1953–54, Renuka served as the president of the AIWC. After Satyen's death in 1969, she kept herself busy with work, which became her primary outlet. She concentrated her energy on the Women's Coordinating Council, which was a body of various women's organizations.

In 1988, Renuka was conferred the Padma Bhushan, the country's third-highest civilian award, for her contribution to public service. She died on 11 April 1997 in Calcutta. She had a life extraordinaire. She was not swayed by power or positions. Renuka never abandoned her principles.

13

SAROJINI NAIDU

At nine, her father insisted she speak only in English – something she resisted. One day, he locked her in a room to force the habit. After that, she only spoke to him in English. Not just that, she mastered the language – authored several poems and plays, and just at twenty-six, she was a literary sensation, an unofficial cultural ambassador of India.

But why all the fuss about the English language? What happened to the Indian languages? Why was there a shift among privileged Indians to learn the colonisers' tongue? It was all started in 1835, by British politician T.B. Macaulay, when he declared that English would be the official language of India instead of Sanskrit and Persian (the official language of the Mughal Empire). The British introduced English in India hoping to create a group of people who could act as interpreters and messengers for them. Over the next decades, there did emerge a class of

Indians that enthusiastically took to English. This young woman was one of them. But contrary to their objective, she deployed her mastery over the colonial language to fight against the British Empire. She was their fiercest critic – giving it back to them in their own language. Little did she know that when she grew up, she would be titled 'Nightingale of India' for her poetry in English.

Once Upon a Time, a Sarojini Naidu

Sarojini Naidu was born on 13 February 1879 to Dr Aghorenath Chattopadhyaya and Varada Sundari Devi. Her parents were highly accomplished and renowned personalities of their time. Aghorenath was a scholar and social reformer who pursued eclectic interests, such as alchemy. He was the Principal of Nizam College. Her mother was a renowned singer, lyricist and dancer.

Both her parents were devoted to the cause of women's education, economic independence for women, abolishing child marriage and establishing widow remarriage. Her father also advocated for the introduction of the Special Marriage Act 1872 in Hyderabad state. Aghorenath also dabbled in politics. One of the first people to join the Congress in Hyderabad, he helped in propagating the Swadeshi Movement.

Aghorenath and Varada's home was a sanctuary for arts, literature, and a range of other interests and pursuits.

Sarojini was the eldest of eight siblings and described as an overbearing sister who took upon herself 'the right to rule the younger members of the family and the responsibility for things that were, in her opinion, the function of her father and mother'.

Her parents ensured that their children received the best education. They had employed a governess to teach them English and French. Sarojini was a prodigal talent; she was an excellent student despite her lack of interest in formal tutoring.

Aghorenath was also keen on inculcating in Sarojini a scientific temper and steered her towards a career in mathematics or science. But the poetic instinct she inherited from her parents, proved far stronger. When she was thirteen, she wrote 'Lady of the Lake,' a 1,300-line poem, in six days, as well as a drama. She did this just to spite her doctor while she was ill, as he told her to not touch a book.

Top of the Tops!

Sarojini was sent to Madras to appear for her matriculation examination. She topped the Madras Presidency, earning her fame throughout the country. For three years after this brilliant performance, Sarojini was confined to her parents' home in Hyderabad as she was unwell. During this time, she interacted with a number of visitors from all walks of life who frequented the Chattopadhyaya residence.

An Uncommon Love

It is likely that at one of the gatherings in her home she met her future husband – Dr Govindarajulu Naidu, a young doctor who had just returned from England after studying medicine at the University of Edinburgh. Sarojini was smitten. Sarojini and Naidu's love met with resistance from both their families, as the couple belonged to different castes and because, at sixteen, she was still too young. The same year, Sarojini wrote a Persian play, a copy of which was sent to the Nizam of Hyderabad, Asaf Jah VI. The Nizam was greatly impressed by her talents and granted Sarojini a generous scholarship to pursue higher studies in England. Sarojini sailed to England in 1895. She attended classes at King's College in London and later joined Girton College, University of Cambridge. The exposure and the education turned her into a mature poet. In 1905, she published her first collection of poems, *The Golden Threshold.*

Unfortunately, her health deteriorated in the damp British climate. To recuperate, she left for Switzerland and then Italy. In 1898, Sarojini returned to India and married Naidu in December. They registered their marriage under the Special Marriage Act, 1872, the same legislation that Aghorenath had helped implement in

Hyderabad. Theirs, in fact, was one of the earliest recorded cases of inter-caste and inter-regional marriages in the country. The couple settled happily in Hyderabad and had four children: Jaya Surya, Padmaja, Ranadhira and Leilamani.

Power of Positivity

Sarojini's struggle with her health continued but she remained cheery and focused on her writing.

Sarojini was the life of parties and always dressed in bright colours. Renuka Ray once said, '*Sarojini Naidu was there and with her wit and charm she kept everybody in roars of laughter and was the presiding deity on the occasion.*'

Women Cannot Write Poetry?

Sarojini had become an international literary sensation after the publication of *The Golden Threshold*. The collection was a bestseller and received rave reviews from newspapers and journals alike. *The Review of Reviews* magazine wrote, 'This little volume should silence forever the scoffer who declares that women cannot write poetry.' Many hailed it as an amalgamation of the West and the East. Sarojini was hailed as one of the foremost Indian voices. Over the next decade, she published two more poetry collections – *The Bird of Time* and *The Broken Wing*.

A Poetic Orator

At the turn of the century, Sarojini took to social service. She initially worked in Hyderabad, coordinating social and relief work, but craved more. She was invited to speak on different discussion forums across the country. Her speeches touched upon a wide range of issues. Sarojini also campaigned for women's emancipation. In 1902, she addressed large crowds in Calcutta and Bombay, urging women to come out of seclusion, to work and to take up careers. In 1903, at a lecture organized by the Historical Society, Pachaiyappa's College, Madras, Sarojini called on young students to foster a spirit of brotherhood and think beyond region, religion and nationalities. Sarojini shared similar views on nationalism with Rabindranath Tagore, and later in life they became good friends as well.

A Rare Friendship Is Struck

Her speech at the Indian Social Conference in 1906 earned her the appreciation and eventual friendship of Gopal Krishna Gokhale, a senior Congress leader. Their comradeship was based on their mutual love for the motherland and the desire for Hindu-Muslim unity.

Gokhale and Sarojini had great hopes for Muhammad Ali Jinnah in their quest for religious amity. Sarojini shared a deep bond with Jinnah and helped build a group of supporters around him in England. She hailed him as an ambassador of Irish-Indian unity. Unfortunately, in later years, Jinnah dropped his secular ideals and campaigned for India's partition.

Mickey Mouse and the Nightingale

When Sarojini went to meet Gandhi at his dwellings in London, she was amused by the sight of a 'little man with shaven head' who was a household name by then, living like a hermit. She let out an inadvertent laugh, and Gandhi remarked, *'Ah, you must be Mrs Naidu! Who else dare be so irreverent?'* This unusual exchange sparked

Mahatma Gandhi and Sarojini Naidu in London

a friendship that grew into a strong comradeship and a deep, loyal bond. For over thirty years, through their shared work for India's freedom, her dedication never once wavered.

Sarojini and Gandhi worked together till the end. They were a formidable team. She succeeded him as Congress president in 1925. She was a key member of his inner circle, participating in the Dandi March and facing several arrests. Gandhi called her the 'Nightingale of India' and she called him 'Mickey Mouse'. She followed him as a leader but playfully mocked his austere methods, Gandhi enjoyed the camaraderie and her merciless teasing.

An Inspiration to Other Women Leaders

Sarojini inspired women to reach for the sky. She was one of the founding mothers of modern India in its true essence. Sarojini was the northern star for those who wished to serve their country. She influenced the other women in the Constituent Assembly. She led the Congress and emerged as one of the foremost national leaders. Besides fighting for independence, she indefatigably nurtured the feminist movement, mentoring leaders who took over the mantle in later years. Irish–Indian feminist Margaret Cousins called Sarojini 'the brightest star amongst the galaxy of Indian women publicists.'

The Force Behind Voting Rights for Women

The praise of Sarojini's work and growing influence in the fight for women's rights was not exaggerated. Sarojini was the face of the suffragist (voting rights) movement in India. In 1917, she led a delegation of fourteen women to present a memorandum on governance to Edwin Montagu and Lord Chelmsford.

Her vision of a free and modern India was powered by equal rights for and empowerment of women. The memorandum demanded better education, health and maternity services for women along with voting rights.

She made many rousing speeches and made politicians take note of women's rights.

The women of India began to see change. Britain enacted the Government of India Act 1919 which, while having no provision for voting rights for women in the Central legislature, allowed provincial legislatures to enfranchise them. This meant that every province had to take a call on voting rights of women. It was now for the Indian men to step up and stay true to their democratic ideals.

Dark Times

In March 1919, another Act would be passed greatly affecting the basic freedoms of the Indian people, as Britain enacted the Anarchical and Revolutionary

Crimes Act of 1919, popularly known as the Rowlatt Act. The Rowlatt Act conferred on the police far-reaching powers. Provisions of the Act violated principles of natural justice, allowing arrests without warrants, juryless trials and denying the accused's right to know of the evidence against them. Gandhi decided to launch a Satyagraha against the Act. Satyagraha, or a policy of passive political resistance, was Gandhi's biggest flex against British rule in India. Many people were critical of Gandhi's methods. They felt this should be a time for action and not for being passive. There were many Indians who supported British rule in India. Sarojini, however, defended Gandhi.

On 17 March, Sarojini addressed a public meeting in Madras, where she made a forceful case for the repeal of the Act and lent unwavering support to Gandhi's Satyagraha. She said, '*the great law of Satyagraha is the very instinctive law of self-defence against aggression and against tyranny that we Indians have followed.*'

Three weeks later, General O'Dwyer ordered indiscriminate firing on a peaceful crowd that had gathered in Amritsar's Jallianwala Bagh. Hundreds of innocent women, men and children died at the site. The Jallianwala Bagh massacre laid bare the oppression and cruelty of the colonial regime that had till then fashioned itself as a benefactor of the Indian people. Tagore renounced his knighthood in protest. Gandhi and Sarojini too joined Tagore in returning state honours. She gave back the Kaiser-i-Hind, which was awarded to her for her relief work during the Hyderabad floods of 1908.

The following year, Sarojini addressed the House of Commons in England on the massacre. Unsparing in her criticism, she admonished the British for their inhuman treatment of Indian men and women.

Sarojini Is Everywhere

In 1920, Gandhi launched the Non-Cooperation Movement. It coincided with the visit of Edward, Prince of Wales. A welcome procession in Bombay, in his honour, ran into Congress volunteers who pelted stones at the motorcade. Soon riots broke out and it was left to the Congress leaders to quell the violence. Sarojini was one of the people who stepped forward to help make peace.

The movement was withdrawn in 1922 following violence in the Chauri Chaura town of the United Provinces, where a mob burned down a police station, killing twenty-two official personnel. A month later, Gandhi was charged with sedition for inciting violence against the government. He was sentenced to six years in prison but was released early on health grounds. In March 1922, Britain finally repealed the Rowlatt Act.

Madras Makes the First Move

As the fight against the Rowlatt Act was going on, strides were being made when it came to voting rights for women. In 1921, Madras became the first province to grant women the right to vote, followed by Bombay and the United Provinces. Earning voting rights around the same time as their American and some European counterparts – members of 'mature' democracies – is a testament to the perseverance and brilliance of Indian women leaders.

The women leaders did not let up after the initial success. There was still a long way to go. Provinces had said women have the right to vote, but it was conditional. All women could not vote. The right to vote, was based on ownership of property, income and other statuses, which excluded a substantial number of women. In fact, in Bombay, Bengal, and the United Provinces, less than 1 per cent of women could exercise franchise. Further, women still did not have the right to sit in legislative bodies. Indians had been demanding a universal franchise right. The Nehru Report, a draft Constitution, prepared by an All-Parties Conference in 1929, committed itself to equality. It called for equal civic rights for all citizens. Britain was not keen on expanding the right and women's organizations had to consistently struggle for years. It was only with the adoption of the Constitution in 1950 that all women acquired the right to vote.

'We Know We Will Convert You to Our Ideas'

AIWC's work had its share of hurdles but that did not hassle Sarojini. Once a group of young men heckled Sarojini as she took the dais at an AIWC event. They raised slogans of 'Down with the women's social rights'. Disgusted at such bad behaviour, Sarojini made a forceful intervention, forcing the men to retreat. She said, '*If you want to say anything, you must ask me as president to give you an opportunity and to come up one by one to the dais. We are not afraid of you. We know we will convert you to our ideas but only please behave as Indians and cultured gentlemen.*' The front seats that had been occupied by the hecklers soon emptied, to be filled by genuine supporters who had been waiting outside the hall.

Sarojini Naidu *ki Jai*!

In 1925, at the Kanpur session of the Congress, Gandhi proposed Sarojini's name as president. She became the second woman, and the first Indian woman, to head the Congress party. She took to the rostrum amidst scenes of intense enthusiasm and prolonged and loud cries of 'Vande Mataram', 'Allah-o-Akbar', and 'Sarojini Naidu ki jai'. Her presidential address, which was extempore, was delivered in English. She admonished Indians for not doing enough for their country, for their complacency and for merely imitating the ways of the West. The suspension of the Non-Cooperation Movement had created fissures within the party. And Sarojini called for unity under Gandhi's leadership. The speech garnered favourable comments from the international press. The *New York Times* went to the extent of calling Sarojini the 'Joan of Arc' who had risen to inspire India.

What Is in a Flag?

In 1928, Gandhi sent her to the USA to counter 'anti-India' propaganda. Sarojini was also there as an AIWC delegate to attend the Pan-Pacific Women's Conference. During her visit, she addressed multiple meetings across the USA. At the World Alliance for Peace banquet, she noticed that the hall was decorated with flags of all 'free nations'.

She questioned the futility of the talks when India remained subjugated: '*The only guarantee of abiding world peace [was a free India] and till they could hang India's banner dyed in the red of hope, the green of her courage, and the white of her faith among other world symbols of liberty, there could and would be no more peace in the world.*'

The national flag was very meaningful for Sarojini. It was very dear to her. At a peace celebration in New York, she was saddened to see flags of 44 nations but not India's. At an international women's conference in Berlin, on her suggestion, Indian delegates created a tricolour flag from their saris so that their country would not be the only one without the national banner.

These experiences fuelled her passion for India's national flag. She could not wait to see the Flag of Free India created and pushed for it in the Constituent Assembly.

Eventually, when the Indian flag was adopted in 1947, she was jubilant. Saluting the flag of a free nation was a heart-warming moment for those who had toiled for years.

Prison Term

In 1940, Congress launched individual satyagraha. Sarojini went to prison once again, and then again during the Quit India Movement. The prolonged jail terms worsened her health and she left prison on a stretcher. Following her release, she threw herself back to work.

Partition Breaks Her Spirit

As Partition became inevitable, she was despondent. Hindu-Muslim unity had been a particularly important focus area for her, and she was anguished to see her motherland partitioned along religious lines.

In 1946, she was elected to the Constituent Assembly from Bihar. In her first speech at the Assembly, made on 11 December 1946, she said she hoped that the Partition would be stalled. *'I see gaps in this House and my heart is sore because of the absence of those Muslim brothers to whose coming I am looking forward under the leadership of my old friend Mr Muhammad Ali Jinnah.'*

Her speech was one of hope and optimism for the Constituent Assembly.

Sarojini made only one more speech thereafter, on the resolution regarding the national flag. She was appointed governor of the United Provinces, the first woman to occupy the position.

Losing Her Beacon of Light

On 30 January 1948, when Nathuram Godse assassinated Gandhi, all hell broke loose. Stoic in the face of grief, Sarojini made a radio broadcast in Gandhi's memory two days after his death. She recalled his selfless service. She was defiant in grief, urging the listeners to walk his path. *'I say the time is over for private sorrow. The time is over for beating of breasts and tearing of hair. The time is here and now when we stand up and say, "We take up the challenge" to those who defied Mahatma Gandhi. We are his living symbols. We are his soldiers. We are the carriers of his banner before an embattled world. Our banner is truth. Our shield is non-violence. Our sword is a sword of the spirit that conquers without blood. Let the people of India rise and wipe their tears, rise and still their sobs, rise up and be full of hope and full of cheer.'* In Gandhi's passing, she lost a leader and dear friend. For three decades, they had formed a rock-solid partnership, her faith in him never wavering. Shortly after he breathed his last, she put aside her grief and went about preaching his gospel.

Sarojini passed away on 2 March 1949 from cardiac arrest. Sarojini rose to every challenge and inspired countless others. She left a lasting impact on every sphere she touched. Sarojini built modern India and has given the world a life story to emulate. Nehru, then prime minister, paid her a moving tribute in Parliament, '*Just as the Father of the Nation had infused moral grandeur and greatness to the struggle, Mrs Sarojini Naidu gave it artistry and poetry and that zest for life and indomitable spirit which not only faced disaster and catastrophe, but faced them with a light heart and with a song on her lips and a smile on her face... She knew how to sacrifice herself for great causes. She knew also to do that so gracefully and so graciously that it appeared an easy thing to do.*'

Sarojini Naidu making a radio broadcast after Gandhi's assassination

14

SUCHETA KRIPALANI

At fourteen, she may have lacked the courage to openly boycott the Prince of Wales visit to her school, but that incident ignited a nationalist spark in her. Throughout her life, she displayed exemplary courage in standing up to those in power. She had a prolific political career and was Uttar Pradesh's first woman chief minister. She also contributed to rehabilitation of refugees during the Partition and worked tirelessly in riot affected areas. Always principled, she was respected by her peers – even her political opponents. She remained a Gandhian till the end, though initially she did have some hiccups, due to a personal decision. Let's find out more about this firecracker member of the Constituent Assembly.

Books and Brahmo in the Early Years

Sucheta was born to Surendra Nath Mazumdar and Prembala in Ambala (then in Punjab, now in Haryana) in June 1908. Both her parents and their families were followers of the Brahmo Samaj, a reform movement that promoted equality and rejected outdated rituals.

After his medical studies, her father joined the Punjab Medical Service, and the duo set up a home in the state. Since the couple was related to leading Brahmos, their home became a centre of social and cultural functions. All of their nine children received formal education in the leading institutions of the time.

Sucheta, and her sister Sulekha, studied at Loreto Convent in Shimla, after which they were sent to a boarding school in Allahabad. Subsequently, they attended Queen Mary's School in Delhi. She initially struggled with her studies but turned around to become a high-scoring student.

First Brush with Nationalism

Sucheta was fourteen when she had her first brush with nationalistic activity. In 1921–22, Edward VIII, the Prince of Wales, was on a royal tour of India. The students at Queen Mary's School were scheduled to welcome the prince in Delhi. However, the royal tour had come only months after the gruesome Jallianwala Bagh massacre. Sucheta and Sulekha were outraged at the thought of standing in honour of the Crown in whose name the killings were carried out. At the same time, they couldn't refuse to join the welcome party and decided to be absent during the event. Being absent made them feel ashamed, that they lacked sufficient courage to refuse to honour the prince.

The Joy of Khadi

Following the Jallianwala Bagh massacre, the Non-Cooperation Movement was launched by Gandhi in 1920, which renewed the patriotic fervour in the people. Fuelled by the spirit of Satyagraha, Gandhi's philosophy made its way into the Mazumdar home. Inspired, Sucheta took to khadi. She was joyous when she got her hands on her first khadi sari. She had her first 'Gandhi darshan' in 1924 in Delhi. For a young woman like Sucheta, seeing Gandhi was an exhilarating moment. She shared, '*We waited, all elation and excitement, in a crowded room, having a look at the great man! Little did I then imagine how close to him I would get one day!*'

A Rough Patch to Overcome

Despite having a window into the world of freedom fighters, Sucheta was focused on her education. She topped the intermediate examinations, winning a gold medal and a scholarship. She wanted to pursue medicine, but it was ruled out by her father.

By then, the family had moved to Lahore, and Sucheta and Sulekha were enrolled in Kinnaird College for Women. Tragedy struck the Mazumdars when Sulekha, who was diagnosed with rheumatic fever and heart ailments, passed away. Her untimely death marked the beginning of a rough patch for the family.

Surendra Nath couldn't bear the loss of his daughter; he became seriously ill in 1927 and passed away two years later. The family's savings had been all but exhausted on Surendra Nath's treatment, and after their father's death, Prembala moved the family to Delhi, where they rented a small flat.

Passes with Flying Colours

Despite the tough times, Prembala ensured the children received a good education. Sucheta, who had graduated from the Government College for Women in Lahore, enrolled at St. Stephen's College for her Master's in history. The only woman in the class, she was picked on by her male classmates. The titters died down when she outscored them in all but one paper. Continuing with her stellar academic record, she graduated at the top of her class and earned another gold medal.

Torn Between Family Duty and Nationalism

Sucheta's completion of studies coincided with key national events. The Simon Commission had been formed by the British to review the Government of India Act 1919 and suggest governance reforms. But there were no Indians on the commission, and Indians thought the review would be biased and a fruitless exercise. They decided to boycott Simon Commission, and the Congress along with other parties prepared a draft constitution. This was popularly called the 'Nehru Report' and listed far-reaching reforms. It claimed dominion status for India, proposed fundamental rights for all citizens and a parliamentary system along with universal adult suffrage.

Next, in December 1929, the Congress passed the Purna Swaraj resolution that called for complete independence. Gandhi launched the Civil Disobedience Movement through the Dandi March. While the Congress followed Gandhi's non-violent methods, there was a clamour for the revolutionary overthrow of the British government. Things heated up when three young revolutionaries, Bhagat Singh, Sukhdev Thapar and Shivaram Rajguru, murdered a British police officer. They did this to avenge the death of Lala Lajpat Rai, a prolific leader who was killed when he sustained injuries from a lathi charge while taking part in a peaceful protest against the Simon Commission in 1928. All three were convicted and awarded the death sentence.

This caused an uproar. Sucheta was working as a teacher when the three were sent to the gallows. The hangings led to an outpouring of emotions and a huge procession joined the families for the last rites. The anti-British atmosphere was rising and the people of Lahore acted as if shaken by a storm. Sucheta was itching to join the freedom movement but was held back by familial obligations.

A Sincere Commitment

From Lahore, Sucheta moved to Banaras Hindu University (BHU) as a lecturer in history at the Women's College. The position provided Sucheta with financial stability, and a year later her family moved in with her. At BHU, she interacted with Jivandas Bhagwandas Kripalani, a follower of Gandhi and Congress leader, who was on a tour to popularize khadi. She was greatly impressed by his intellect, and they formed a close friendship. Kripalani would often call on her whenever he visited Banaras.

After the January 1934 India–Nepal earthquake, the region of Bihar suffered several casualties and devastation. Congress leaders, including Kripalani, converged in the state to assist with relief operations. He encouraged Sucheta to join them. She took leave from the university and followed Kripalani to Bihar. The relief work was her first experience working in a rural setting. Sucheta was shocked by the extent of poverty and inhumane conditions. The relief work brought her in close contact with Gandhi, as well as Jamnalal Bajaj, an industrialist (founder of the Bajaj Group) who was overseeing the work. Bajaj was impressed with her and asked her to leave BHU and join the Mahila Ashram in Wardha, in modern-day Maharashtra. Sucheta made a trip to Wardha but declined the offer. She was put off by the rigidity and puritanical beliefs of Vinoba Bhave, a prominent Gandhian activist. The rigid beliefs at the ashram were endorsed by Gandhi and almost cost Sucheta her blossoming relationship with Kripalani. Gandhi feared the marriage would distract Kripalani from the freedom cause.

But they were both united in their desire to see a free and prosperous India. Over time, the couple's bond only grew stronger. They decided to marry. They also decided not to have any children, such was their commitment to the cause. Eventually, Sucheta and Gandhi made peace with each other and formed a solid partnership.

Paving Her Own Path

Free from familial obligations, Sucheta was keen on starting political work, but initially Kripalani dissuaded her. He didn't just want her to be his assistant – he felt she was capable of much more. He urged her to follow her own bent of life and to grow independently.

Despite the differing views on Sucheta's role in politics, the couple always shared a deep respect for each other's work. Their professional and personal lives were intertwined.

After independence, Kripalani quit the Congress to form the Kisan Mazdoor Praja Party (KMPP), Sucheta joined him. In 1956, Sucheta left KMPP and returned to Congress. Now, husband and wife were on opposing sides in Parliament. This invited ridicule from several people. Kripalani noticed the awkward situation as people were not accustomed to spouses having different political opinions. To his credit, Kripalani stood firmly behind Sucheta. When a minister taunted him saying that 'even his wife does not agree with him', Kripalani made it clear that he valued her as an equal partner.

Starting All-India Mahila Congress

Sucheta's political journey started at the grassroots, when she joined as a worker at the ward level in Allahabad. Later, she took charge of the foreign affairs department. One of her more lasting legacies was the formation of the women's wing of Congress, now known as All-India Mahila Congress. The department's goal was to raise the political consciousness of women and position Congress as the vehicle of social change. Gandhi's active encouragement created more space for women in politics. Sucheta left no stone unturned and travelled from state to state for the task. The lack of finances was a major concern. The provincial units were reluctant to set aside money for the new department. This mammoth project was put on hold after her arrests in 1940 and 1944.

Sent to Prison

In 1940, the Congress launched individual Satyagraha in response to Britain's unilateral decision to make India a party to World War II. As the war was raging, plans to organize a mass movement were replaced with an advocacy programme. Under the individual Satyagraha plan, Congress workers would go to the people and preach against the war. Sucheta, who was selected to offer Satyagraha at Faizabad in United Provinces, was promptly arrested. She was sentenced to a year in prison.

Meanwhile, the Congress upped its ante by demanding absolute freedom from British rule. On 8 August 1942, its leaders passed the Quit India resolution in Bombay. Both Sucheta and Kripalani were in attendance. To quell the protest, the police started arresting Congress leaders. As Kripalani was being taken away, he told Sucheta to not go back to Allahabad and instead oversee the work in Bombay. Thinking on his feet, he specifically asked her to avoid the United Provinces. Sucheta managed to escape arrest because the warrant had been issued in the United Provinces.

Underground Movement

The key task before the workers who had escaped arrest was to ensure party activities did not suffer due to the detention of the entire senior Congress leadership. Sucheta and other Congress workers went underground and created a separate cell, known as the Central Directorate. The Central Directorate would send propaganda bulletins and other information to the All-India Congress Committee (AICC), from where it was transmitted to workers. Offices were set up in various locations in Bombay. The underground group collected information, raised finances and assisted workers who were in trouble with the authorities. By September 1942, a few activists had even organized an underground radio station, called the Congress Radio, to counter government propaganda transmitted through the All-India Radio (AIR). The radio started with a nightly programme that was broadcast at 8.45 p.m. The bulletins comprised national news and talks by freedom fighters. The location of the underground station had to be constantly changed, and the broadcast team worked closely with Sucheta. The broadcasts were made by Usha Mehta, a student-activist with immense courage. Sucheta feared that the radio team was going to be discovered by the police and wanted to stop the operation. She didn't want to put Mehta's life at risk. The Congress Radio remained active till November 1942, when it was unfortunately seized.

Mehta was arrested along with the other organizers and was sentenced to four years' imprisonment.

Master of Disguise

Although Congress was committed to non-violent means, the pent-up anger amongst some workers and the public led to violence and sabotage of government property. The police came down heavily on these dissenters.

With a warrant out for her arrest, Sucheta had to steer clear of the authorities and take on guises to evade them while travelling around the country to coordinate Congress activities. Although she was usually very careful, she was ultimately arrested in Bihar. She was sent to Lucknow Jail and this time categorized as a 'dangerous prisoner'. She was released in 1945.

Getting Independence at Any Cost – A Moral Dilemma

Years later, Sucheta Kriplani recalled feeling disheartened during the Quit India Movement due to debates over violent and non-violent approaches. After meeting Gandhi in prison in 1943, she shifted towards non-violence, despite facing criticism. The choice between violence and non-violence was a huge moral struggle, influenced by her youthful enthusiasm to expel the British from India at any cost.

Gandhi Sends Her to Rural India

After Kasturba Gandhi's death in 1944, Gandhi formed a trust to address the issues of women in rural India. After her release from prison, Sucheta went to meet Gandhi and he asked her to take on the work of the trust, which involved travelling across India and working in villages. She was reluctant as after a long time she and Kripalani were getting to spend time together; Kripalani had been in jail since 1942 and Sucheta was either underground or imprisoned. On the side, Gandhi pushed Kripalani into getting Sucheta to accept the offer, till she finally agreed. The trust's work brought her close to Gandhi again.

Sucheta Kripalani addressing a crowd

Devastation of Direct Action Day

In 1945–46, elections were held for the Central Legislative Assembly and provincial assemblies. Congress formed governments in eight provinces and was in majority at the Centre. The Muslim League formed governments in Bengal and Sindh and stepped up its demand for Pakistan, a separate nation for India's Muslims. Muhammed Ali Jinnah, the leader of the Muslim League, declared 16 August as Direct Action Day and proclaimed, '*We will have either a divided India or a destroyed India.*' Direct Action Day was a call to arms, leading to large-scale riots in Bengal. Shortly, the violence spread around the country. In Noakhali in Bengal, organized violence broke out against Hindus who were in the minority. There were reports of mass killings and looting. The government was indifferent to the plight of the victims, claiming no conflict in the region. Hearing of the devastation in Bengal, Gandhi announced that the Congress president would visit the area and prepare a report, adding, 'if need be he would die there'. Kripalani, then the Congress president-elect, rushed to Noakhali, with Sucheta beside him. She had insisted on accompanying him as she feared he was in harm's way. They undertook a quick survey of the violence-affected areas. The Hindu residents were scared for their lives and narrated harrowing tales of gruesome violence and forced marriages of young women. Kripalani returned to Delhi to submit his report to Gandhi, while Sucheta stayed back at the request of the residents. To help the survivors get back on their feet, Sucheta started relief and rehabilitation centres, setting up camps.

No Freebies

In November, Gandhi visited Noakhali. He was distressed by the carnage he witnessed. He also instituted some changes in the relief work. Gandhi wanted to do away with the camps. He argued that once the Congress workers left, the Hindus had to fend for themselves, and the camps weren't going to be a long-term solution. Secondly, he advised Sucheta not to give out food without asking people to do some work in return. Gandhi explained that simply handing out free help could take away the poor's sense of dignity. When Sucheta hesitated, saying it would be hard to expect a poor mother with a baby to work, Gandhi urged her to stay firm and encourage everyone to contribute in some way, even if the task seemed small.

The Voice of Refugees

In April 1947, Sucheta accompanied Kripalani on a visit to Kashmir to meet Sir Hari Singh, the Maharaja of Jammu and Kashmir. They travelled via Lahore and Rawalpindi and heard tales of great distress and communal unrest. Fearing the unknown, a mass migration was underway, as Hindus and Sikhs were travelling towards the east and Muslims to the west of Punjab to find safety. Sometimes, these communities would be faced with violence, and often women and children would bear the brunt of it. On their way back, Sucheta decided to stay put at Rawalpindi. She toured the areas hit by communal violence, making detailed notes of the testimonies. On her return to Delhi, she informed Gandhi of the disturbing events. He was aghast and told her that he had no inkling of the intensity of the cruelty. She forwarded her report to the press, in the process earning reprimand from Sardar Vallabhbhai Patel, the minister in charge of internal security, who felt that the publication was going to fuel conflict in Delhi. Delhi had become a centre for the refugees fleeing the communal frenzy in Punjab.

Hindus and Sikhs from Pakistan arrived in Delhi in large numbers. As a result, the Congress formed a committee to oversee relief work for refugees. Dr Rajendra Prasad was appointed chair and Sucheta the general secretary. Sucheta brought immense energy to the task and mounted an effective relief operation within days. She became the voice of the refugees in Parliament, advocating for just compensation and rehabilitation. A few years later, she was at the forefront of the relief work during the arrival of the Tibetan refugees in 1959. In 1971, she helped raise funds and organize support for refugees fleeing East Pakistan.

Contribution to the Making of the Constitution

Her involvement with relief work did not leave her with enough time for an active role in the Constituent Assembly. One major intervention she made was when the legislative assembly was discussing the Hindu Code Bill. She spoke in favour of the Bill, highlighting how it stood for equality. When Kripalani broke away and formed a new party, KMPP, as he was disillusioned by the Congress, Sucheta joined KMPP and contested the first Lok Sabha elections from New Delhi and Gorakhpur. She won from New Delhi, but the party fared badly. In fact, Kripalani himself lost his seat. The detractors of the Congress came together and formed a single party. Sucheta was elected leader of this group, and she found herself in the Opposition.

In her first speech at Parliament, Sucheta castigated the government for its failures and lack of vision. She felt the government was being complacent and showed no urgency in dealing with the different challenges facing the nation.

Sucheta was an effective opposition leader, keeping the government on its toes and raising the voice of the marginalized. Her criticism of the Congress continued outside Parliament as well.

Does a U-Turn!

Sucheta's first term in the Lok Sabha came to an end when her term was annulled in 1955 on some technical grounds. Sucheta rejoined the Congress despite having been so critical of Nehru, the Congress party and the government just a few months before. Sucheta justified her decision to return to Congress by her desire to do constructive work, not just criticism. She wanted to work, not merely talk.

Unsurprisingly, her return to the Congress earned her some uncharitable remarks. Her supporters were annoyed with her for going back to a party that she so strongly condemned in the past.

The Kings Meet the Kripalanis

In 1959, Sucheta played host to American civil rights activists Martin Luther King Jr and his wife, Coretta Scott King. She was then the vice-chair of the Gandhi National Memorial Fund. The Kings visited Sucheta and Kripalani for lunch. A year later, the Kings joined Sucheta and Kripalani as they embarked on a lecture tour in the USA. The Indian couple led training camps organized by the Student Nonviolent Coordinating Committee (SNCC), a civil rights group. Their visit to the USA brought together activists from different generations to use Gandhi's ideas about non-violence to fight for racial equality.

Becoming Chief Minister

In 1961, Uttar Pradesh Chief Minister Chandra Bhanu Gupta (also known as C.B. Gupta) invited Sucheta to join his Cabinet. She was appointed minister for labour, industry and community development. Two years later, Sucheta became the chief minister. As the first female chief minister in India, Sucheta proved to be an able administrator. She focused her energies on governance, paying special attention to improving the irrigation network in the state. She invited industrialists to invest in the development of Uttar Pradesh, offering them incentives. However, she could not manage the internal politics, and this took a toll on her health. Sucheta continued to be active in public life for as long as she lived. Sadly, her health deteriorated even more as the years passed.

A Star No More

In 1974, she tragically died of a heart attack. She was survived by Kripalani who continued to lend support to democratic causes and lived long enough to see the first non-Congress government assume power in 1977 after the Emergency.

Sucheta ultimately joined the pantheon of selfless leaders that created history and dedicated their lives to striving for a progressive nation. The *New York Times* paid obeisance to her, 'a leading fighter in the struggle for Indian independence'. Sucheta was admired for her idealism even by her political opponents. Prime Minister Indira Gandhi called her a 'person of rare courage and character. She brought credit to Indian womanhood.'

15

VIJAYA LAKSHMI PANDIT

A life of privilege does not mean a life without problems or challenges. But it does give you a platform – to fight for yourself and others who may find themselves in similar situations. Vijaya Lakshmi did just that. Though born in a progressive family, she wasn't spared the injustices of her times. Her brother got a formal education while she was home-schooled. Later on in life, due to outdated succession laws, she had no access to her husband's property or income after he died. These first-hand experiences made her a life-long women's rights activist. She ardently believed that there can be no freedom for India without equal rights in all spheres for women. Always a go-getter, she used her voice and diplomatic skills to contribute to changing social laws and building a modern India.

She was a tireless freedom fighter and a feminist activist who donned many hats in the service of her country. She was India's representative to the world. As ambassador to the USA, and the USSR, and the high commissioner to the UK, she helped implement and mould India's foreign policy agenda. Often overshadowed by her sibling, she quietly shattered glass ceilings – across the nation and on the world stage.

Where It All Began

Born in Allahabad to Swarup Rani and Motilal Nehru in August 1900, Vijaya was initially named Swarup Kumari. The first of two daughters, she was younger than Jawaharlal by eleven years and elder to her sister, Krishna, by seven. She was lovingly called 'Nanhi' (Hindi for little one); the nickname was shortened to 'Nan' by her European governess, a name that stuck.

Motilal was born in 1861 and had never met his father, who had died before he was born. For a while, the family fell into tough times, but quickly overcame the odds. Motilal's mother, Indrani, was a remarkable woman who taught herself to read and write, and raised the family in traditional Kashmiri customs. Motilal joined the legal profession and set up practice in Allahabad, the seat of the high court. Within a decade, he was renowned for his intellect and hard work, and was amongst the highest-paid lawyers of the time. As he ascended the legal profession, Motilal bought a bungalow in the elite

Civil Lines area in Allahabad, then inhabited exclusively by European families. The lives of the Nehru clan were transformed. European governesses were recruited for the young children's education; knives and forks found their way to the dining table. It is believed that Motilal declared that only English was to be spoken in the house. His dress and mannerisms were increasingly Western, and his outlook liberal.

Abode of Happiness

Swarup was born at a time when her father Motilal bought another massive property in Allahabad. Motilal named the building Anand Bhawan (abode of happiness). Motilal was fond of the Western lifestyle and spent lavishly to maintain the same. He fostered good relations with the British in Allahabad. Anand Bhawan became the venue for countless dinners and teas for senior government officials. The Western lifestyle and the intermingling with the British initiated them into a cosmopolitan world, providing them with ready access to differing views and cultures. In fact, at the housewarming party, a high-ranking British official hoped that the house 'would become the cement holding together the British Empire'. Ironically, Anand Bhawan went on to become a central location in the struggle for India's independence after Motilal gifted it to the Congress.

Paradox of Progressive Views

Despite Motilal's affluence and progressive views, Swarup was not granted formal education. Even her homeschooling by private tutors invited taunts from orthodox people, outraged at the freedom she had been given. Swarup yearned

Vijaya Lakshmi with her brother Jawaharlal Nehru

for a university degree, which, in her view, was a passport to opportunity, and was disappointed with her father when her brother was sent to London for higher education.

A World View at Home

The atmosphere at Anand Bhawan compensated for some of the disparity created by the gender divide in terms of education. It was perhaps at the gatherings at Anand Bhavan that both Jawaharlal and Swarup imbibed the crafts of diplomacy – Swarup more so, as she stayed on while Jawaharlal went to London for his studies. She was instilled with self-confidence, a quality which served her well when she was required to put across her views forcefully when people held different viewpoints.

First Lesson in Patriotism

With Motilal's growing involvement with the Congress, their home, Anand Bhawan, became prominent in the field of politics. This gave Swarup a front row seat to observe and understand the national developments. From an early age, she knew of the affairs of the country. There was constant hustle and bustle in her household, with many people streaming in to discuss politics with her father. She was in close proximity to people who became India's greatest freedom fighters.

ALWAYS INTERESTED IN THE WORLD AROUND HER

Young Swarup's interest in politics was not restricted to domestic affairs. She followed with an emotional interest the Easter Rising of 1916 and the Irish Home Rule Movement – a campaign for self-government in Ireland. The same year, she attended the Lucknow session of the Congress, and was mesmerized by the speeches of Annie Besant and Sarojini Naidu.

The Irish Home Rule Movement inspired Indian leaders to start a movement of their own (Home Rule League) under Annie Besant and Bal Gangadhar Tilak. Though Swarup was too young to join the League, she nevertheless volunteered at its Allahabad office.

Packed Off to Sabarmati

It was in 1916 that she first met Gandhi, but things did not go well initially. Though Swarup was involved in politics, she was still a young girl with thoughts of romance, and known to be impulsive. She shocked everyone in the family, by secretly marrying Dr Syud Hussain, who had been appointed the editor of *The Independent*, a newspaper founded by Motilal. An ardent follower of Gandhi, Hussain belonged to an aristocratic family from Dacca. The young editor had taken up residence in Anand Bhawan. This was where he first met Swarup and, after a brief courtship, got married. For Swarup, it was perfectly natural to marry outside her religion. However, the marriage was annulled after Motilal refused to bless the union.

Soon after, Hussain left for England and devoted his years abroad towards the freedom cause. He remained a bachelor.

Back at Anand Bhavan, in a bid to keep her focussed, the Nehrus decided to send her to Sabarmati Ashram.

Swarup, so far brought up in luxury, found Sabarmati to be very austere. At the ashram, everyone was expected to partake in household activities and food was sparse. The spartan living conditions and an unduly strict moral code – left the young Swarup unimpressed. She joined the league of those who respected Gandhi for his ideals but were not keen on adopting his ways.

Satyagraha, Gandhi's philosophy of holding onto truth and frugal living, eventually found its way into the Nehru household. The Jallianwala Bagh massacre, where a British general opened fire on an unarmed gathering, had shaken the country. In a remarkable step for one of the richest lawyers of the time, Motilal, also the Congress president in 1919–20, plunged into practising Satyagraha and boycotted the Western lifestyle. The lavish lifestyle at Anand Bhawan became a thing of the past.

Shaadi in Khadi

Sometime in 1920, Ranjit Pandit, a barrister from Gujarat, who was a follower of Gandhi, visited Allahabad to consult Motilal on a case. On meeting, Swarup and Ranjit took a liking to each other. Ranjit was smitten and, on his third day itself at Anand Bhawan, he proposed marriage. The family approved.

The wedding festivities went off smoothly. The only hiccup that arose was when Gandhi insisted that the bride wear a khadi sari and no jewellery, which was unthinkable for a wealthy Kashmiri Brahmin family. Swarup's mother strongly opposed the idea, but Gandhi's will triumphed in the end. When the couple went to him to get his blessings, he apprised them of their duty to the country and urged them to strictly abide by the Gandhian philosophy.

Not Everyone is Happy

Newlyweds Vijaya Lakshmi Pandit and Ranjit Pandit settled in Rajkot with the groom's family. Vijaya's in-laws were not too pleased with the match, as they felt that the association with the Nehrus was going to hinder Ranjit's career prospects. In 1920, after Gandhi's call for non-cooperation, many Indians withdrew from activities that sustained the British Empire. Just as the parents predicted, Ranjit decided to give up his legal practice and plunged into the freedom struggle.

Working Together

The Non-Cooperation Movement saw people burning imported goods, a symbolism that Vijaya found to be a waste of resources given the scale of poverty in the country. Nonetheless, she joined her husband in setting up spinning and weaving centres in villages around Rajkot. Their home became a centre for Congress's constructive program, where they founded schools and developed programmes for the Harijans and other underprivileged people. Even after the movement was called off in 1922, Vijaya and Ranjit continued their work in Rajkot. In 1926, they moved to Allahabad. The couple had three daughters: Chandralekha, Nayantara and Rita.

Prison Time and Personal Loss

Vijaya was an enthusiastic participant in the Congress activities in Allahabad. She helped organize events, led processions and delivered speeches against the British Raj. In 1930, the Congress launched the Civil Disobedience Movement and the authorities responded by detaining party leaders. This time, Ranjit was also put behind bars, along with her father and brother. This was a big blow to the Nehrus. The prison term damaged Motilal's health, and he died in 1931 after a bout of illness. A year later, Vijaya was arrested for leading an Allahabad City Congress Committee meeting. She was also sentenced to rigorous imprisonment for a year. After some time, Vijaya was moved to a jail in Lucknow, which was an eye-opening experience. While there, she was exposed to caste and class barriers. She wondered how her fellow inmates, who were also freedom fighters, could have progressive ideas, yet simultaneously hold on to selected conservative practices.

Mid-Day Meals and More

In 1934, Vijaya contested the elections for the Allahabad Municipal Board, forging ahead in her political career. She was successful and was made the chair of the education committee. Vijaya took to administration like a duck to water. She convened regular meetings with teachers, patiently hearing their grievances. In meetings with the Board, she called for greater funding for the 'milk scheme', which entailed providing undernourished children with diluted milk. Vijaya called for expanding the scheme – one of the first recorded cases of a mid-day meal programme designed to improve the nutrition standards of children. Faced with low budgets, she decided to crowdfund the initiative and the milk scheme she envisioned eventually saw the light of day.

After the enactment of the Government of India Act 1935, the British announced elections in the provinces. This meant that power was now divided between the centre and the provinces or states. Congress registered handsome returns, winning 758 of the 1,500 seats, and was able to form government in seven provinces.

In these provincial elections, Vijaya had won a seat in the United Provinces Assembly from Kanpur. Although she was against joining the government, she was appointed minister and given charge of local self-government and health, becoming the first woman in India to be elected to a Cabinet position. When she assumed office, healthcare services were in shambles; she noted that no minister wanted the health portfolio. However, she gave her best to the task at hand, and increased the budget allocation for healthcare, laying emphasis on developing maternity and childcare services.

Also, in 1937, the first order of business that came her way was moving a resolution demanding the repeal of the GOI Act 1935 and the formation of a Constituent Assembly.

Calls Out Hypocrisy

In 1939, Britain made India a participant in World War II. It caused an uproar in the provinces, with Congress governments condemning the decision, because they were never consulted on the matter. At the United Provinces Assembly, Vijaya denounced Britain's policies and urged Indians to come together to fight for freedom. She called out Britain's hypocrisy in subjugating India while claiming to fight a righteous war. Vijaya saw through the design of the British 'divide and rule' policy, and urged others to put aside their differences and work towards the common goal of complete freedom.

Vijaya was also actively involved in the women's movement, and her nationalist agenda complemented her

DOES MEDIA TREAT MEN AND WOMEN EQUALLY?

Vijaya's criticism of the British was not restricted to the affairs of the state. She did not mince words when calling out the press for its gender bias. Despite her hard work and drive, it was often her appearance that elicited the first questions from journalists. She compared her press experience with that of her brother, which was dramatically different from hers. 'I think of the interviews I have seen my brother give. What straight, clear, and intelligent questions are put to him, and yet I, who also attempt to do public work, am treated as if my interests were confined to clothes and children and those petty social activities in which the lady of means and leisure engages in order to allay the prickings of her conscience,' she fumed.

Vijaya had a perceptive mind regarding gender issues. She saw clearly how the education system deepened gender stereotypes – raising boys to be dominant and girls to be dutiful.

goal of gender equality. She was a part of the AIWC and was elected as its vice-president in 1938 and president in 1941–42. She used her position to urge women worldwide to unite on the platform of non-violence. She used the platform to make speeches against the British government and their hypocritical ways.

Protests Fall on Deaf Ears

The British government had paid no heed to India's protests regarding participation in the World War II. This resulted in Congress leaders resigning from the provincial governments. The party announced the launch of individual Satyagraha. Vijaya too joined the movement and was sentenced again, this time to four months' imprisonment.

In August 1942, Congress launched the Quit India Movement. Shortly after the launch, Vijaya returned to prison on 12 August 1942. At 2 a.m. that night, seven truckloads of armed policemen came to arrest her in Allahabad. She immediately knew that the movement would mean multiple jail terms for the Congress leadership. In 1943, Vijaya and Ranjit decided to send their children to the USA, as they felt that the tense political situation in India was not conducive for their studies. She saw off her daughters in Bombay while she was on parole, and headed straight to jail. This must have been a testing time for the Pandit family. Both Vijaya and Ranjit, lodged in the same jail, found time for each other, exchanging notes at times and singing together. In her diary entry on 27 April 1943, she hopes that Ranjit would not be transferred to Bareilly.

Her worst fears came true when Ranjit was transferred to the Bareilly prison, and eventually died there, after being denied timely medical attention.

Fight For Your Right

Ranjit's demise was not just a personal loss for Vijaya. It brought her face to face with the outdated succession laws that would leave her penniless and fighting in court for her rights. The absence of a direct male heir and a will meant that Vijaya and her daughters had no claim on his property. To make matters worse, Ranjit's family refused to provide Vijaya with a share; her brother-in-law went to the extent of freezing a joint bank account in the name of Ranjit and Vijaya.

The fighter that she was, Vijaya filed a case to claim a share, although senior lawyers told her that she stood no chance in a court of law. Gandhi came to her rescue and helped negotiate a compromise with her in-laws. Her case drew a lot of attention and was widely reported. It ignited demands for reforms in Hindu laws to ensure equality between men and women. The conservative section resisted the move, calling it an interference in religious affairs. Ultimately, the Hindu Succession Act was enacted in 1956 and gave the wife, mother and direct descendants precedence in succession, over other family members.

The Act was amended in 2005 and now allows married daughters a share in ancestral property.

Off to the USA

On her career front, after Ranjit's death, Vijaya's workload increased. She headed for Calcutta to help with the famine relief effort and raise funds for children. Gandhi wanted her to travel to the USA, to inform the Americans of how the British were oppressing Indians. Congress leaders

A STRANGE TRAVEL STORY!

In January 1945, there was a conference in the USA to discuss Asia's future post the World War. Vijaya was to represent India at this conference, but her passport had been confiscated and there was little hope of the government reissuing it. After some hectic back-channel discussions, the Americans came to her aid. She was offered a seat on a USA Army transport plane. Her travel on an army plane sans passport was believed to have been facilitated by President Roosevelt himself. Once in the USA, she was reunited with her daughters who were studying there. Wherever she went, she was greeted by huge crowds. Vijaya's tour was a success, but she wasn't done yet.

were hopeful that the USA would put pressure on Britain to allow independence for India. This was a morale boost for her, and she readily agreed.

Who Gets to Represent India?

In 1944, the USA, the UK, the USSR and China proposed the formation of an international organization – what is today the UN. Representatives of the four countries, along with several other nations, met in San Francisco in April 1945 to finalise the details of the proposed organization. Vijaya was very vocal about who gets to represent India. Not an India as seen by the British, but an India represented by an Indian. Eventually, she was appointed as head of the Indian delegation for the UN General Assembly session of 1946. Vijaya was the first woman to head a country's delegation. At the UN, she led India's case against South Africa's mistreatment and denial of human rights to Indians residing there. The General Assembly passed a resolution noting the mistreatment of Indians. While India won the vote by a two-thirds majority, it did not lead to any positive change for the residents in South Africa.

Her time in the USA equipped Vijaya with the skills to become a diplomat-par-excellence. Soon after the UN session, she came back to India, where she was elected to the Constituent Assembly. In her first and only speech, she recalled moving a resolution in 1937, demanding the formation of a Constituent Assembly:

'It was my privilege in 1937 to move the first resolution... in my Province, demanding a Constituent Assembly to draw up a constitution for an independent India. Today, ten years later, that Constituent Assembly is meeting here. This is a historic milestone in our progress toward freedom, and yet, Sir, freedom remains just a little beyond our grasp.'

Always a Diplomat

In August 1947, Vijaya was appointed India's ambassador to the USSR and moved to Moscow. Her two-year stint there kept her away from many sessions of the Constituent Assembly. In 1949, she was appointed ambassador to the USA, and she was, in fact, the first woman ambassador. Vijaya received a warm welcome in the USA. She was a recognized face in Washington, and Americans were hopeful of stitching a key partnership. She oversaw Nehru's first visit to the USA and negotiated a generous wheat loan when India was facing a famine. Vijaya also went on to become the high commissioner of the UK. She was at her diplomatic best in both the USA and the UK. In 1953, she was elected president of the UN General Assembly, the first woman and the only Indian to occupy the office. For nearly two decades, she was India's most recognizable face on global platforms. Nehru told her he wanted to appoint her as India's vice-president but changed his mind later. Instead, in 1962, she was appointed the governor of Maharashtra. The same year,

Vijay Lakshmi Pandit, US President Harry S. Truman, Jawaharlal Nehru and Indira Gandhi

she was conferred with the Padma Vibhushan in the civil service category. After Nehru's death in 1964, she won the by-election to the vacant Phulpur seat, her brother's constituency. She won again from Phulpur in 1967, but differences with her niece, Indira Gandhi, forced her into early retirement. The aunt and the niece once shared a strong bond, but it deteriorated after Indira became the prime minister in January 1966.

She remained deeply concerned by the growing personality cult of Indira. When Indira imposed the Emergency in June 1975, her aunt became one of her fiercest critics and may have been put under surveillance.

Vijaya was a champion of liberty and self-determination for nations and their people. Blood relations did not come in her way of striving for causes she held dear. It is to the credit of leaders like Vijaya Lakshmi Pandit that India managed to survive challenges and thrive as a democracy.

Her life is perhaps best described by the code word sent in the telegram to her father in Paris to announce her birth: 'Tempest'. Vijaya Lakshmi Pandit's tempestuous life tossed her into prison from the comforts of a luxurious home. The prison also took her father and then her husband away from her. After years of struggle for freedom, she charted India, a young democracy, to a stable course. She even came out of retirement to stand up to authoritarianism, doing her part in guiding the country back to the constitutional framework. In December 1990, at the ripe age of ninety, this illustrious leader breathed her last in Dehradun, at the foothills of the Himalayas.

ACKNOWLEDGEMENTS

The journey of *The Fifteen,* the book on which this adaptation is based, started in 2018. Since then, different people came together to bring to life the stories of the remarkable fifteen women.

We are grateful for the immense support we received from friends, family, editors, reviewers, and most importantly, the readers of *The Fifteen.*

In our interactions with readers across cities, they usually expressed a desire to see an abridged version for a younger audience. Thanks to the editor, Sanya Verma, and the team at Hachette India for their foresight to begin the adaptation process quickly.

Thanks to Vidya Nesarikar who adapted the book for a younger audience, in such a short duration of time.

**TO ACCESS THE COMPLETE BIBLIOGRAPHY,
PLEASE SCAN THE QR CODE BELOW:**